the book of

NO

250 Ways to Say It—and Mean It—

and Stop People-Pleasing Forever

—— *Susan Newman, Ph.D.* ——

McGraw·Hill

New York   Chicago   San Francisco   Lisbon   London   Madrid   Mexico City
Milan   New Delhi   San Juan   Seoul   Singapore   Sydney   Toronto

Library of Congress Cataloging-in-Publication Data

Newman, Susan.
    The book of no : 250 ways to say it—and mean it—and stop people-pleasing forever / Susan Newman.
       p.   cm.
    ISBN 0-07-146078-0
    1. Assertiveness (Psychology)   2. Interpersonal communication.
3. Interpersonal relations.   I. Title.

BF575.A85N49   2005
158.2—dc22   2005018273

1 2 3 4 5 6 7 8 9 0 DOC/DOC 0 9 8 7 6 5

ISBN 0-07-146078-0

McGraw-Hill books are available at special quantity discounts to use as premiums and sales promotions, or for use in corporate training programs. For more information, please write to the Director of Special Sales, Professional Publishing, McGraw-Hill, Two Penn Plaza, New York, NY 10121-2298. Or contact your local bookstore.

This book is printed on acid-free paper.

*For the millions of people who find themselves in millions of places
doing millions of things they don't want to be doing
because they couldn't say no*

Other Books by Susan Newman

Nobody's Baby Now:
Reinventing Your Adult Relationship with Your Mother and
Father

Parenting an Only Child:
The Joys and Challenges of Raising Your One and Only

Little Things Long Remembered:
Making Your Children Feel Special Every Day

Little Things Mean a Lot:
Creating Happy Memories with Your Grandchildren

Little Things Shared:
Lasting Connections Between Family and Friends

Getting Your Child Into College: What Parents Must Know

Let's Always . . . Promises to Make Love Last

Don't Be S.A.D.:
A Teenage Guide to Stress, Anxiety, and Depression

It Won't Happen to Me:
True Stories of Teen Alcohol and Drug Abuse

You Can Say No to a Drink or a Drug:
What Every Kid Should Know

Never Say Yes to a Stranger:
What Your Child Must Know to Stay Safe

Memorable Birthdays:
Now a Guide, Later a Gift

CONTENTS

Author's Note

Yes, I Need This Book

When I mentioned to my friend Julie that I was interested in exploring why people have so much trouble saying no, she instantly pointed her finger at me and raised her voice, "*You* need this book." What does she mean? I thought. I can say no with the best of them.

Not minutes later, the phone rang and my husband said he needed his gym bag that he left by the door so he could work out at lunch. Would I bring it to him, immediately? Did I say, "No, I'm working on Chapter 3 and don't want to stop"? Did I say, "No, send a messenger or pick it up on your way to the gym"? Did I say, "No, I'd rather walk the dog, thank you very much"? I did not. I said, "Sure, honey," dropped everything and then snarled at him over dinner.

I had never thought of myself as a person who acquiesced and agreed to do whatever was asked of me. I knew I was always overwhelmed by commitments—both personal and business—but it hadn't sunk in that my situation was the result of my own inability to say no. After talking to Julie and acting as my husband's messenger, I realized that I was programmed to be accommodating and repeatedly fell into the trap of involving myself in situations I could so easily avoid by simply refusing. I had to learn to deal with the guilt that frequently accompanies denying what often seems a modest request. But guilt, I quickly discovered, was only a small part of the problem. There's generally much more going on when someone asks you a favor beyond the favor or task itself.

I started paying attention to what was being asked, how and when it was being asked, and how quickly I was responding—usually too fast in an effort to please. Over the last year or two, I kept track of my own and others' yeses. Saying yes was not something I carefully considered. I was easily worn down or coaxed into agreement. Mainly, I was troubled by the possibility of upsetting someone if I refused. I needed to learn that saying no didn't tilt the world on its axis, cause my husband not to love me, my friends to abandon me, or my colleagues to ignore me.

I've been practicing. I've learned to spot a snow job from a salesperson and weaseling from contractors. I know pretty fast when a relative attempts to start my guilt-meter running or a friend manipulates me in a direction I don't want to go. You will, too. I've compiled a list of questions and demands I should have said no to, and I have every hope that you also can quickly adapt to living happily ever after with no as a staple in your vocabulary.

This book was not created to justify the egomaniac who wants everything his or her way. Rather, it's for the all too many of us who too often say yes when the circumstances don't really require compliance. Its lessons will strengthen your resolve so you have time to include—and do more for—the people and things most important to you.

INTRODUCTION

The No *Word*

W hen Rodgers and Hammerstein wrote the song "I Cain't Say No" for the popular Broadway musical *Oklahoma*, they were definitely on to something.

"Yes." "Sure." "No problem." The words are out of your mouth before the reality or the enormity of the commitment you make registers. You realize too late that you don't want or don't have the time to do what you've taken on. You neither wish to babysit a friend or sibling's difficult or delightful children, nor do you have time to walk someone's pesky dog. You wonder how you got roped into an extra office assignment or the arrangements for a coworker's farewell party. How does this happen to me so often? you ask. If you're not wondering, maybe you should.

When you were two years old, you had little difficulty shouting, "No!" but slowly the word *no* was drilled out of you. The more you said no, the angrier your parents got.

Your teachers found *no* unacceptable. If you said no when you were older, you were afraid of losing a parent or friend's loyalty or love. No doubt, some of that apprehension has carried over into your adult life.

The word you repeated without the slightest hesitation at age two is problematical, if not impossible, in many of your interactions today. Most people have been programmed to think *no* carries a strong backlash. As you will find out, the risks of refusing are not as scary or damaging as you believe. In fact, *the damage done by saying yes indiscriminately affects you much more than your refusals affect the people you turn down.*

Yes-people become weighed down, feel torn, trapped, or taken advantage of, and as a result are unhappy or annoyed with themselves for being easy marks.

Many label that millisecond it took to agree as a weak moment: I was having a bad day, I was in a bad mood, I didn't feel well, my guard wasn't up, and a long list of other excuses. How does this happen? You may be a "born giver." You've been helping out all your adult life, aiding the "born recipients" or "takers," who thrive being on the receiving end. Being cared for is what the takers in your life have come to expect.

Another reason for incontrollable yeses is the inability to think clearly about what is being asked. What keeps you from saying no is usually right below the surface of the question—an implied challenge, an unspoken guilt-producing *should*, your own hesitation to offend or disappoint, your fear of the asker's power or perceived hold on you. There's also the gray area filled with those things you have no strong feelings or opinion about. In the gray zone you're wishy-washy and undecided. Requests that come out of the blue can leave you floundering in the gray zone. Until you pause long enough to analyze a situation, you will continue to be a yes-person—annoyed with yourself and often annoyed with the person you couldn't say no to.

You may be a person who has to be pushed and prodded, have your back to the wall, or be on serious overload, angry with yourself and those pressuring you before the thought of saying no enters your mind. When you've agreed so many times that you've reached the breaking point, your *no* may come out as snide and hurt the relationship. Even when the relationship stands unscathed, a brusque *no* can leave you feeling unhappy with yourself for being snippy or appearing indifferent.

After committing, doubt sets in: when do I have time to organize a fund-raiser or help my friend move? You may feel insecure if you've agreed to something beyond your abilities. The looming questions then become: How do you wiggle out of whatever you've consented to? What real excuses do you have? Are you going to hedge or blatantly lie? Extracting yourself is a complicated, frequently less-than-truthful process. Consider what you put yourself through: anguish, maybe deception, and an array of negative emotions that could have been avoided by giving a straightforward *no*.

You may be in the habit of saying yes without opening your mouth—you've acquiesced to someone else's wishes because you simply couldn't focus on what you wanted—what you wanted for breakfast, where you wanted to go on vacation, what time to meet, what movie to see. By not speaking up, by not making your preferences known, you essentially say yes.

Volunteering and promising fall into the category of saying yes as well. You might not say the *yes* word, but you entangle yourself in commitments just the same. You can tell when you've done this because the recipient of your good deed looks astonished or spews forth with an embarrassing number of thank-yous.

For so many people, saying yes is a pattern that they would like to—and can—break. If you start keeping track of the times you agree over a week, you'll begin to realize the need to say no more often. How frequently have you wished you could simply blurt out, "No" to someone requesting your time, your talent, your energy, your muscle, your money, your thoughts, your support, or merely your presence? The mind and body can take only so much stress. Doing endlessly for others taxes and compromises your health.

If you find yourself in places doing things you don't want to be doing, it's time to begin figuring out what would make your life easier and more pleasurable. A touch of aggressiveness may be the only tool you need. But you can't assert yourself or voice your preferences until you know what they are.

Stepping into *No*: The Basics

There are five basic steps to keep in mind to hone your ability to turn people down. As soon as you begin to apply them, you will start to feel justified saying no and you will see results. You won't be able to say no to everything asked of you, nor will you want to, but you don't have to be an ever-accommodating yes-person to be loved, respected, and admired.

1. *Make a list of your yeses over the period of a week.* If you are an inveterate yes-person, the number will shock you. The acceptable number will be different for everyone. One request could send you into a tailspin, while it might take four or more to set off someone else. The real gauge is how pressured, tight for time, or resentful you feel. Any negative reaction— Why did I agree? What was I thinking? What am I doing? I don't want to be available, I would rather be elsewhere—is the true measure.

2. *Pay attention to how you parcel out your time.* If most of your time is monopolized assisting one friend, when will you see other friends? If family or job demands are high, what's left over for your own enjoyment? When your time is well managed, you'll keep some in reserve for what's most important to you.

3. *Get your priorities straight.* Who has first crack at you without your feeling burdened or anxious? A child? A boyfriend? A girlfriend? A spouse? A boss?

4. *Know your limits—start to define them if you don't know what they are.* They can be emotional or physical or both, but there's a point at which your line is crossed. How much of other people's problems can you tolerate without feeling drained? How long are you willing to put up with one-way friendships with you always on the giving end? Because you're not a trained therapist, decide how personal you're willing to be and what kind of requests make you uncomfortable. On the physical side, when does your stamina give out? What requests are too taxing? To stay healthy your body and mind require rest to rejuvenate, and if you don't set limits you won't get it.

5. *Give control to others to ease your responsibilities.* When you don't trust others to be in charge or to get things accomplished, you wind up agreeing to and doing far more than your share of what someone else could be doing. Eliminating the need to run things yourself to be sure they turn out the way you like them relieves much of the pressure you put on yourself.

Rarely is a request as straightforward as it appears, and many of the difficulties you'll face in responding are complicated—at least it feels that way. You could fear damaging a friendship, hurting a parent's feelings, disappointing a boss, having a child say, "I hate you." Yet the more often you refuse, the more quickly you'll learn that the fallout is less extreme than you imagine. Once you accept these realities, the easier it is to say no.

No: A Learned Skill

Saying no may be completely uncharted territory—you're a master of *yes*, a novice of *no*. For you, saying no means trying something entirely foreign. Think of the process as an adventure into the unknown with delicious bounty at the end of the journey—a calmer life with you supervising it.

While saying no probably won't change your personality, it will help you assert yourself when you want to and put an end to that empty feeling in the pit of your stomach when you commit beyond your stamina or to the point of draining your emotional reserves. Having *no* at the ready creates boundaries and keeps others from crossing them. Begin with caution, assessing who it is in your life you need to stand up to and using a few refusals here and there as a testing ground.

A word of caution: Do not gild your *no* with a lie or pad it with lame excuses. That's counterproductive because in all likelihood you will feel guilty about your fabrications and that's precisely what you are trying to avoid.

You might choose to build your *no* muscle with friends, and after reading Part 1, "With Friends," you'll be able to meet them head-on. If it's your family that pulls you into all things imaginable, you'll want to focus on Part 2, "All in the Family." If your failure to say no is most prevalent on the job, then read Part 3, "At Work," to learn scripts to use with your boss, a coworker, or anyone in between. Finally, delve into Part 4, "Really Difficult People," to master *no* with service and repair persons and an array of salespeople.

Parts 1 through 4 are filled with scenarios, questions, and demands that snag people every day. While the requests may not be precisely ones asked of you, you will recognize the situations and predicaments and be able to put yourself into them.

Each question, favor, or demand is then dissected into three parts: What's going on here, Response, and Alert.

* **What's going on here.** Warns of possible manipulation and trickery or offers details of the circumstances that could influence your answers. This information helps you analyze what's being asked and why you may be having a hard time saying no, so in similar situations you can decide realistically if you are being taken advantage of and if you wish to comply. "What's going on here" will build your resistance and help you assemble a strong base from which to begin your turnaround.

* **Response.** Once we've broken down the motive behind the question, this part will extricate you and, in most instances, suggest language to disengage you from the commitment without your seeming uninterested or impolite. When you aren't confident that you can find the words on your own, the scripts give you the words to say no. The "Response" also helps you assess the situation and teaches you to be less impulsive when answering. For instance, you will learn that before answering with a yes to anybody, you

must think critically about the request and ask yourself the following questions:

—Do I have the time?
—Will I feel pressured to get it done?
—Will I be upset with myself?
—Will I be resentful of the other person?
—Will I feel duped, had, or swindled?
—What do I have to give up to do this?
—What can I gain? (What's in it for me?)

Answering these questions before agreeing will help you create a new mind-set. Over time and with practice, *no* will become your first option instead of the current, deeply ingrained propensity to say yes that emanates from, among other things, wanting to please, wanting to be liked, needing to be needed, being timid, avoiding confrontation, not knowing your rights, or feeling, plain and simple, that you should.

✳ **Alert.** This provides rationale and words of caution so the next time you're in a similar bind you'll hesitate before locking yourself in. The "Alert" also reveals what people who ask favors think, why they behave the way they do to get you to do something for them, and in certain cases why you react as you do—and that knowledge gives you the ammunition and courage to say no and not obsess over the decision.

Some approaches to *no* may seem hard-edged, but they are realities of life. They are truths about others and ourselves that we don't want to accept and facts about human nature that are difficult to acknowledge. An important lesson to learn from the start is this: *People don't think about you as much as you worry about what they think.*

Saying *Yes* to the *No* Word

You've seen them do it, triumphant athletes pumping their arms in elation at their successes. When you say no, you'll find yourself raising your arms like a champion and shouting, "Yesss!" to yourself. When that happens often enough, you succeed at keeping your boundaries secure.

In the beginning, think of each "should I or shouldn't I" as a practice session. Like any other skill, the first few tries are the hardest, but at least you are hesitating, and that's progress from your usual impulsive, agreeable self. After that, turning people down will become noticeably less difficult.

Think no before you think, "No problem, I'll do that for you."

Sometimes it takes being trapped to mark your territory, but start practicing until you can call up a *no* when you want it. You may falter at times, but don't be too hard on yourself. The person you said yes to will be back at some point, and you'll be ready to say no the next time because saying no relieves a tremendous amount of life's tension and aggravation.

Each time you agree when you don't want to, you give up a piece of yourself. You begin to feel powerless because you are in another person's grip, fulfilling her wishes or meeting his needs and not your own.

By saying no, you voice your opinion, stand up for your rights, and become sole proprietor of your life.

For many people, saying yes is the story of their lives. They find themselves volunteering to work on a fund-raiser, and the next thing they know they're running the fundraiser. They attend a PTO meeting and are roped into becoming PTO president. Their mothers are bored or lonesome, their friend needs a ride, and those prone to *yes* make themselves available. They fear people will decide they are lazy or uncaring if they decline, but wind up not having lives of their own. Taking the time to learn to say no is not only a huge gift to yourself but also to everyone else in your life.

The *No* Credo

As you become proficient at saying no, these rights will become standard operating procedure. This credo significantly reduces any trouble you might have. It is your bill of rights to the freedom and life you deserve.

You have the right to:

* Make your feelings and desires known
* Establish and guard your personal boundaries
* Keep your needs in the forefront so saying no is possible
* Exercise your power and choice to say no
* Repeat *no* until you are heard
* Use *no* to get your life in control and to be in control of it
* Weigh the fallout of saying no
* Request the details before committing
* Postpone an answer; stalling for time is your prerogative
* Refuse anyone who insists on an immediate answer
* Turn down those who flatter or attempt to con you into a yes
* Withhold explanations in an attempt to soften your *no*
* Avoid tasks beyond your ability or expertise
* Alter a request to make it—or part of it—manageable
* Suggest someone else or offer an alternative solution
* Say no initially and change your mind later if you wish

1

With Friends

The very definition of *friend* makes saying no to one extremely difficult. Before deciding whether or not to deny a friend his or her request, make the distinction between who is a true friend and who is an acquaintance, between a friend with whom you have a balanced give-and-take relationship and one who takes advantage of your good nature or your availability. Seriously consider a smaller, more elite group of friends made up of only those who truly care about and support you. You have less of an option weeding out family members, but with friends you can be choosy.

Who's a Friend?

Realizing that friendships have different levels of depth, duration, and feeling, the core elements that apply to most friendships are concern and caring, support and trust, mutual respect, acceptance, respect of privacy, and ability to listen. But don't expect one friend to meet all your needs or that you should meet all of his or hers. Because people and how they interact change, friendships should be reevaluated on a regular basis.

Friendships continually evolve—or erode. Sometimes a friend who can be counted on in your smaller circle and who follows the ground rules most of the time begins to expect too much. You want to be helpful, but when the friendship is lopsided and not reciprocal, you have to take a stand. You'll want to say no to those who always ask for your assistance but are never there when you need them. Be leery of acquaintances passing as friends when you're deciding whether or not to say yes. It's simply not possible to be all things to all people.

Saying no will not turn you into a bully or make you insensitive or petty. You won't stop helping others, but you'll become more discerning about how you respond and to whom. By being more selective about the demands you respond to, you'll protect your health, have time for yourself, and have time to assist only those you want to help— real friends whose friendships you want to preserve.

At times you may feel boxed in, as if you have no choice, but remember: *you always have a choice.* If you take your time before you commit, you are more likely to judge the situation and be able to offer an unqualified *no.* You don't need to give lengthy explanations or excuses. *No* is simply no.

Saying no to casual friends and acquaintances also becomes simpler when you think about what's good for you and stop worrying about what someone else thinks. People have surprisingly short memories, particularly when it comes to insignificant events in their day-to-day existence. In probably ninety-nine out of a hundred instances, your *no* is tossed off because the asker almost immediately focuses on finding someone else. Only you carry the weight and worry—topped with a couple scoops of guilt. It's time to hang up your guilt and use your time and energy more wisely.

When *No* Is Crystal Clear

Ever wonder why people gravitate to you when they need something done? Is it because you do so many things well or because you appear to have the time? More likely it's because they know they can count on you to say yes, to go out of your way to please them even when it means squeezing the task in, rushing other things, or skipping something you might have scheduled or wanted to do.

Being a chronic yes-person wins only modest, temporary accolades and sometimes little praise. People who expect you to be there for them often forget to be appreciative and begin to take you for granted. The encounters and dilemmas in the scenarios that follow will help you discriminate between what is a real need and what is only presented as such and help you determine how you can be useful without being overly involved.

The Scenario

"Will you write another letter to my landlord? I don't know what to say, and I've been trying to write it for days."

What's going on here: Careful, the helpless approach can catch you every time because growing up you were taught to help a friend in need. Your first thought is how can I let this person down when she needs me, but you've already written four letters for her. She's playing to your intellectual side and abilities, and you're buying.

Response: "No." Verbally give your friend a few essential points to include in her next letter to get her started.

Alert: When left to their own devices, those who portray supreme incompetence usually figure out what to do.

The Scenario

"Will you help me put this bookcase back together before my company arrives tomorrow? When I repair something it looks ready to be carted to the dump. When you do it, it looks brand-new."

What's going on here: Your friend is flattering you to engage your skills. You haven't had this much praise since you mastered tying your shoelaces. It's your ego that wants to say yes to keep the compliments coming, but you've seen the bookcase, and it will take more than a day to get it in shape to hold books safely. Rein in your ego before you respond.

Response: "Thanks for the compliment. It's a big job, but you can do it. You underestimate your ability."

Alert: Be leery of being turned into an instant expert. Flattery can catch you off guard and quickly get you to say yes. Return a compliment with a compliment to shore up the other person's confidence.

The Scenario

"I hate to ask you, but when you're in the store could you pick up a few things for me for dinner? I've got a list right here."

What's going on here: If she truly hated to ask a favor, she wouldn't. How can you refuse? You are going to be in the store anyway. You've been raised to be an accommodating person; the idea that nice people say yes and terrible people say no has been pounded into your head. Normally you would buy what's needed and drop it off, but today you're in a hurry and don't have time for an extra stop.

Response: "I wish I could, but I can't today."

Alert: Protect yourself and still be perceived as a thoughtful person by using an empathetic tone when you refuse.

◯ The Scenario

"Will you drop this package off at Gordon's for me? It's on your way."

What's going on here: Not on the way exactly. To go to Gordon's you have to take a different, more trafficked route home, and there's often nowhere to park in his neighborhood. You can figure twenty minutes driving around to find a spot. If he's not there, you can't leave the package on the stoop, so you will be responsible for it overnight. And if he is home he'll involve you in a lengthy conversation. It's impossible to cut Gordon short, he's a talker. You feel you should do it, but you don't want to deliver the package.

Response: "No, I'm going in the other direction today."

Alert: Stop measuring your self-worth in terms of what you do for others. You probably have done or will do many favors for this friend.

◯ The Scenario

"Will you rearrange the cabinet for me? Be sure you put the glasses on the bottom shelf and the bowls where I can reach them."

What's going on here: From the start, this request has conditions. You're helping a finicky friend who will change your arrangement as soon as you're out the door. She's just looking for someone to keep her company, and you have better things to do.

Response: "No, it's better if you do this yourself; you know exactly how you want it done."

Alert: Fastidious and perfectionist friends will manage to find something wrong with what you do or how you do it.

The Scenario

"I have two tickets for the opening of the new play at Graham-Bell Theatre for tomorrow night."

What's going on here: Pretty straightforward—you've been invited to attend a play. *The hitch*: you don't like the subject matter, heavy drama, or either of the leads.

Response: "Thank you, it was so thoughtful of you to invite me. I really prefer musicals. Maybe Ali or Seth or Graham would like to go; they like dark drama."

Alert: You don't have to like everything friends like to keep them in your circle or to be in theirs.

The Scenario

"Come with me. I hate going alone."

What's going on here: What you thought was a long-buried fear of loneliness has been resurrected. You remember when as the new kid in the class you were ignored, when you weren't picked for kickball in the third grade, when you weren't invited to someone's birthday party, when you were the last one to go out on a date, and all the times you went to the movies alone. You're reliving the loneliness of your youth. Times have changed: you're not left out or alone anymore.

Response: "No. It's not possible for me to go with you."

Alert: Be aware when childhood issues trigger old feelings and taint your judgment.

◯ The Scenario

"Please call my date. Tell him I'm sick and can't see him tonight."

What's going on here: Your friend is in fine health but has decided for reasons you may or may not know that she doesn't want to keep this date. You haven't told a successful lie in your life. It's not worth the shame you feel when you're caught.

Response: "No, I can't lie for you."

Alert: Don't agree to do someone else's, even your best friend's, dirty work.

◯ The Scenario

"Can I borrow that cashmere thingy you wore to Lana's party?"

What's going on here: We're all taught to share. It's a virtue right up there with patience and cleanliness. If you have lent items in the past, a friend will expect you to hand it over without a blink. She has her own clothes, yet she often wants to wear yours. If you say okay, you'll be watching her in your new sweater, worrying about the underarm stain she might leave or the spots she might add. You won't enjoy yourself.

Response: "I haven't decided what I'm wearing." You can also say, "I paid a fortune for that and I'm not lending it, not even to you."

Alert: Lending items precious to you is beyond the call of friendship. You don't have to share everything.

The Scenario

"You have such a good eye. Can you come over for a few minutes to help me rearrange the furniture?"

What's going on here: Your friend could legitimately need an extra pair of hands to lift the heavy pieces. But some people ask for one thing and give you the "while you're here" story, getting you to do something else. You could be there hours longer than you planned. Ask exactly what has to be moved and how long it will take.

Response: "Wish I could, but I can't."

Alert: Should you decide to help, be very specific about the amount of time you have.

The Scenario

"Sam just stormed out. I need you this minute."

What's going on here: Your friend sees you as the voice of reason, the person who can make sense of the breakup and make her feel better. She doesn't hear you tell her you're in the middle of cooking the first dinner for your in-laws or that the doctor told you to stop driving because you're nine months pregnant and can hardly get out of a chair. She persists. Your company may soothe her for the moment, but the real pain will return the minute you leave her. Stopping what you are doing and rushing over immediately will not ease her distress, as you know from her endless breakups.

Response: "No, I can't come over right now, but I'll call later to see how you're doing." Be very sympathetic.

Alert: No one, certainly not a friend, can erase the pain of someone else's dissolved relationship. She'll sort it out in time. With persistent or manipulative people, you will have to repeat your *no* until they hear it.

⬤ The Scenario

"Will you show me how to use my new computer?"

What's going on here: On the surface, a half hour of computer instruction appears quite doable. Seemingly manageable requests have a way of escalating out of proportion into time-consuming commitments: phone calls with questions about lost files, malfunctioning Internet connections, viruses. All that can go wrong likely will, especially if you're dealing with someone who normally requires a lot of hand-holding.

Response: "No, I think you'll learn faster from a professional. I really don't know enough."

Alert: Pay attention to what is being asked to be sure you fully understand the magnitude of the job and any residual problems that will demand more of your time.

◯ *The Scenario*

"Hope I didn't wake you, but the screen just froze on the computer I bought from you. Do you know what I should do?"

What's going on here: You thought you were being a good guy; you gave your friend a stellar price on your old computer, and she thinks because you once owned it you are responsible for its performance for as long as she owns it.

Response: "I'd like to help, but I don't know. It's midnight; call tech support."

Alert: When you sell a computer, a car, or an appliance to a friend or relative, make it clear that you don't provide round-the-clock customer service.

◯ *The Scenario*

"I forgot I was in charge of snacks for our get-together tonight. Can you pick up something on your way over?"

What's going on here: Your disorganized friend wants you to take charge, meet her obligations for her—very annoying because she didn't forget this one time, she forgets every time.

Response: "Can't, I'm running really late."

Alert: It's not your job to bail out a friend who regularly flies by the seat of her pants.

● *The Scenario*

"Hear me out, just once more?"

What's going on here: It's a sad, but not tragic, story that you've heard at least a dozen times before. Your friend is wallowing in whatever her current crisis is, and she's telling anyone and everyone who will listen. She knows she's overstepping her bounds when she says, "just once more?"

Response: Be kindhearted: "I know you're hurting and this is a problem, but rehashing it with me is of no use. I can't make it better."

Alert: If she's such a good friend and feels she can bare her soul to you repeatedly, she is also capable of understanding that you don't want to hear her sob story again and again.

Getting Personal

When friends feel they are your bona fide confidants or protectors or you are theirs, saying no may be your only means of self-protection. You'll want to be cautious, too, when you respond to issues that relate to them more than to you. In very personal situations such as love interests, finances, how you or they dress or wear your hair, you need to understand a "good" friend's motivation *and* your own to be able to hold your ground.

● *The Scenario*

Your friend sternly advises you to get rid of the most recent man or woman in your life.

What's going on here: Could be your friend sees something not endearing that you can't or don't want to acknowledge. Could be that she honestly believes he "drags you down." It could just as likely be that your friend resents the time you spend with him leaving less time for her. You want to carefully weigh if your friend is merely looking out for her own interests (having more of you) or if she may be jealous.

Response: "Thank you for trying to protect me."

Alert: Worry about the quality of friendship you have with people who selfishly try to be the architects of your love life.

● *The Scenario*

"You would look a lot younger if you colored your hair. Have you thought about it?"

What's going on here: Your friend is giving you her point of view, one you may not agree with. You don't want to be bothered with the time-consuming maintenance once you begin coloring your hair, and you're not unhappy with the gray. Rather than come back with a barb or show your annoyance with her for implying you don't look so great, be gentle. She'll get the hint that she's gone over the line.

Response: "Thanks for the suggestion, but I like the gray."

Alert: A friend will very likely back off when she realizes that you don't appreciate her beauty tips.

◯ *The Scenario*

"Can I count on your donation?" Or, "You'll up your donation from last year, right?"

What's going on here: If a friend is asking you for money, he knows you're a generous person. In fact, you gave to his charity last year when he caught you off guard and pressured you to the point of saying, "I'll send a check." To him you are a sure bet, and every contribution he gets makes him look better with the other fund-raisers.

Response: "I'm giving to the women's shelter this year. I believe in what they are trying to accomplish. I know your group does valuable work as well, but I feel connected to the local shelter." Or, "I can't swing it this year" (if true).

Alert: Your friend's charity isn't necessarily yours.

◯ *The Scenario*

"Can you spot me a fifty? You know I'm good for it."

What's going on here: You'd like to oblige to underscore what a good friend you are. However, lending money can put a wedge in a friendship and make it uncomfortable for both of you. Think about how you feel when you buy a friend's lunch or movie ticket and she, although she promised, doesn't remember to reimburse you. Stung enough times on the small stuff, you're in a good position to project how it will feel and how angry you'll be when you lend big money. Make it a policy not to lend money to friends— you'll keep them much longer.

Response: "No, I'd love to, but I'm strapped" (if true). Or, "No, I don't lend money to anyone. That's how I am." Or, "I don't think our relationship should involve money."

Alert: Lending money is one of the quickest ways to make a good friend an ex-friend.

◯ *The Scenario*

"Let's hit the mall on Saturday."

What's going on here: You love this friend dearly and have lots in common, but not shopping styles. You know what you want, find it fast, and buy it. She touches every garment in the store, tries on half of them, and then agonizes over whether or not to buy. Usually, she doesn't.

Response: Tell her the truth. "You and I can't shop together; you drive me nuts."

Alert: Shopping with someone whose speed and approach don't match yours promises to be a long, excruciating process, one you surely want to skip.

◯ The Scenario

"Can I borrow your car?"

What's going on here: Your friend may be in desperate need of a car, but how much will his or her borrowing inconvenience you? Lending your means of transportation is asking a lot. What will you do if after your friend's use, it needs to be repaired? Can you get by without your car? If this is a recurring request, consider the following before consenting: Is the car always returned with a full tank of gas? Is it as clean as it was when it left you? Is the borrower appropriately appreciative?

Response: "No, sorry, but my policy is never to lend my car." Or, "I can't give up my car; I'm too dependent on it."

Alert: "Neither a borrower nor a lender be, For loan oft loses both itself and friend." —William Shakespeare

◯ The Scenario

"Should I wear a paper bag until it grows out?"

What's going on here: You're in murky waters—if you say you love your friend's haircut when you don't, your friend may know you are not being truthful. To ease her obvious distress at having chopped off all but an inch of her hair, it's best to keep your answer light.

Response: Laugh appreciatively, then firmly just say, "No."

Alert: When it comes to the touchy area of physical appearance, play it safe when responding to loaded questions. It's too easy to hurt—and to be hurt.

◯ *The Scenario*

"Ed is going to kill me if he sees our credit card bill. Can you help me pay it off or at least reduce it?"

What's going on here: Your friend has piled up outrageous charges. She's desperate to hide her "sins" before her husband discovers them. In all likelihood, you are not the only person she's asking to bail her out.

Response: "I want to help you, but there's no way I can."

Alert: You are not responsible for a friend's extravagant spending habits or poor budgeting, nor should you want to get involved in her deceptive marriage. As much as you would like to protect her, allow her to deal with the consequences and perhaps she will curtail her spending in the future.

◯ *The Scenario*

"I'm feeling fine. Want me to walk a straight line? One more drink and then I'll get going."

What's going on here: He's been guzzling beers all evening at your house, and you're concerned about his driving. He doesn't appear drunk, but you know from the quantity he's consumed, he's had too much. This is serious enough to forgo diplomacy. You can try to make him wait an hour or so before he leaves. The delay will send him the message that you are not backing down.

Response: "No. I'm cutting you off for your own safety."

Alert: If he hurts himself or anyone else you may be legally responsible.

◯ *The Scenario*

"Do you think I should marry David?"

What's going on here: While you may think David is the worst mistake of your friend's life, keep that thought to yourself. She could well wind up married to David, and you and she will see little, if any, of each other in the future. She won't forget what you said.

Response: "That's up to you. Only you can honestly know what you really want and what makes you happy."

Alert: Offering opinions on someone's marital choice has ended many lifelong friendships.

◯ The Scenario

"Sam is mad at me. We had a fight and now he doesn't think he wants to go on vacation with us. Can you talk to him for me?"

What's going on here: Sidestep this one immediately. You're not a counselor, and you don't want to play one for Sam or your friend. When you act as a peacemaker, you end up spending hours listening to both sides of the story and delivering declarations that they could more efficiently tell each other.

Response: "No, the two of you need to work this out yourselves."

Alert: When you're a middleman, you run the risk of statements being misinterpreted and messages getting muddled. You can make the situation worse.

◯ The Scenario

"Don't you think Kevin and Tricia went overboard on their wedding? On decorating their new house? On having such an extravagant first birthday party for their child?"

What's going on here: Be careful. Questions like these are attempts to extract information from you. Innocently revealing what the flowers or the photographer, the house addition or new floor cost could become unpleasant gossip that gets inflated or twisted and back to Kevin and Tricia eventually.

Response: "I haven't thought about that."

Alert: In situations like this, play it safe by playing dumb.

Buying Time

There are some things asked of you that you feel you should at least consider before giving a resounding yes or blatant no. This is the gray area. The questions require you to be indirect or noncommittal, so stay on your toes. You want to digest what is being asked and to think about the outcome of your decision. Stalling tactics work to get you off the hook until you can be certain.

When you hedge a *no*, you buy extra time—time that makes your *no* more palatable and allows you to feel justified about refusing or not providing what the person wants. Given time, you might realize you don't want to be involved, you have no business giving an opinion, or these are people you don't want to help or respond to in any way—realizations that don't pop into your head when you are first approached. And, if nothing else, taking time to think things over makes the other person aware that you have reservations, and that alone may ward off future infringements. Being noncommittal or indirect puts the asker on notice.

● *The Scenario*

"Don't you think I should buy that condo (or new car or stock)?"

What's going on here: You're on shaky ground, particularly if you were unprepared for the question. While you may think highly of the proposed purchase, if, for example, the car is a lemon or the stock tanks, your friendship could be strained if your advice is wrong.

Response: "I don't know." Or, "I'm not entirely comfortable giving my opinion when you're spending your money. In fact, I won't. There's too much at stake and I could be wrong."

Alert: Be guarded in your opinion. In doing so, you tell your friend that you are the wrong person to ask.

The Scenario

"We're going sailing the last weekend of next month. We need you to crew."

What's going on here: You love to sail and enjoy your sailing buddies. The invitation puts you in conflict because a visit with a dear friend from college that same weekend is in the works. You don't want to feel left out, but you also want to see your classmate. If you say no, they'll fill your slot with one phone call.

Response: "Probably not. I have tentative plans with an old friend. I'll have to let you know."

Alert: Best to keep your options open so you don't wind up out on the water when you wanted to be with your friend— or home alone sulking if the visit doesn't pan out.

The Scenario

"Stacey and Hank are joining us, and we've decided to go into town for dinner instead of eating at our house Saturday night."

What's going on here: Without your knowing it, the quiet foursome dinner at your friends' home has become an expensive night on the town. Forget casual, now you'll have to dress, and forget intimate conversation because Stacey's a major gossip. You're disappointed and furious that your friends assumed it was okay to change dinner plans and to include other people without so much as a phone call to you.

Response: "I wish you had let me know you were thinking about altering the evening entirely. Grab your calendar so we can make another date for just the four of us. We don't feel like having dinner in town this week."

Alert: You can let people know you object to their actions without having a huge argument or discussion, and doing so makes them more likely to consider you before changing plans without asking.

The Scenario

"We're totally free the next two weekends to visit. Which one is better for you?"

What's going on here: Are you listening? They invited themselves to your house. If they're that presumptuous,

could be they also need more attention than you are prepared to give. Certain friends are far more demanding than
others in that they like to be entertained, talked to, and not
left alone to amuse themselves. Don't explain what you have
to do or offer flimsy excuses.

Response: "Great idea, but neither weekend is good
for us."

Alert: When inviting people or when they invite themselves
to stay in your home, seriously consider how needy they are.

● *The Scenario*

*"Grab a pencil and we'll go over the trip tonight so I can book
the flights in the morning."*

What's going on here: Your friend is revved up and a great
travel companion. You're delighted to let her do the planning because you don't have time. Your days are crammed
with work and you're exhausted; she leads a far less busy life.
On work days you run out of steam after dinner and want
to crawl into bed. Right now you're so tired you can't possibly focus on vacation details. It requires much more attention than you can muster after ten o'clock at night.

Response: "No, I am absolutely too tired tonight. Let's talk
over the weekend. We can book the flights then."

Alert: You won't get much in the way of rebuttal when you
admit that mentally or physically you can't be effective.

⦿ *The Scenario*

A friend from high school calls out of the blue and suggests you meet for lunch next Saturday. "Can you make it?"

What's going on here: Not the same as attending a high school or college reunion by a long shot; the request means fitting someone else into your busy life. Before you agree, ask yourself whether you have anything in common with this person now. Is there a history you want to revisit or preserve? Is she fun or is she a downer? Were you close years ago? What could she possibly want after all these years?

Response: "I can't meet you Saturday." You can add, "Try me in a few weeks," if you really want to see him or her.

Alert: Don't try to cram someone from your past into your life when you can't think of a good reason to rekindle the relationship.

⦿ *The Scenario*

"Let's put a date on the calendar for lunch or dinner, you name it."

What's going on here: A casual acquaintance has been trying to lock you into a meal for a while and knows you are not particularly interested, so he's giving you the entire calendar year from which to choose. If you make a date, you'll spend a lot of time devising a way to break it.

Response: "I'm really busy and not sure what's coming up in the next month or two. I can't make a date now."

Alert: How you define the relationship is the determining factor. When it's a casual acquaintance, remind yourself that your life is rich with good friends you don't have time to see. If you stall someone enough times, he eventually will realize he's not on your radar screen.

● The Scenario

"I love you. We haven't known each other long, but I want you to marry me. Will you?"

What's going on here: You've been dating a few months and you feel it could work long term, but your sixth sense is telling you that it is too soon for you to make such a life-altering commitment. It's been a whirlwind and you're crazy about him. You need more time to be 100 percent positive.

Response: "I love you, too. Give me some time."

Alert: Unless you are sure right on the spot, hold up. Life-changing decisions can be delayed a few months.

● The Scenario

"Kathryn and Bart are getting married. Let's give them an engagement party at your house, since it's bigger than ours."

What's going on here: In the excitement, you're inclined to agree. It's wonderful that your good friends are finally tying the knot, and they should have a party. On happy occasions such as this, throwing a celebration shindig seems like a great idea—initially.

Response: "Let's talk about it."

Alert: You may well end up throwing the party, but if you take time to talk it through with other friends, you're less likely to be the person in charge or the person handling all the details and expense.

The Scenario

"Will you be in our wedding?"

What's going on here: In the mix of feeling flattered, included, and wanted, bridesmaids and groomsmen accept on the spot without ruminating on what could be major concerns: How close are you to the bride and/or groom? Is the wedding party so large that you speculate if you just made the cut? Can you afford to be in another wedding?

Response: "I'm honored you asked me, but I have to see if I can swing it" (that leaves you open to respond about work commitments or money problems or to decide being in the wedding party is too stressful).

Alert: Before you agree, consider the expense including travel and a special dress or tux or shoes you may not have. Refusing doesn't mean the end of the friendship, but rather it means that you don't feel comfortable for financial or emotional reasons.

The Scenario

"Will you be my maid of honor (best man)?"

What's going on here: She picked you over one of her sisters. It doesn't get more flattering—or shocking—than that. The maid of honor or best man often has a larger financial commitment than the bridesmaids or groomsmen. Tally the responsibilities: hosting a shower, organizing the bridal party, being available to run errands for and with the bride.

Response: "I am speechless to know that you think so much of me, that we are such close friends. It breaks my heart to tell you I can't accept. I would be cheating you if I said yes. I can't do all that needs to be done as well as I think you deserve. It's your wedding, after all."

Alert: Say no when you believe you will be shortchanging the bride or groom and will feel guilty about the duties you want to—but would be unable to—perform.

The Scenario

You both saw the waiter put it there, dead in the middle of the table. She's not making any move to pick up the check, and you don't want to.

What's going on here: You consider yourself quite the generous person, but you repeatedly get stuck with the tab when the two of you eat together. You don't remind your friend how much she owes you because talking about money embarrasses you. Get over it. If and when you go out with her again, tell her before you go that it's her turn to get the check, leave your credit cards home, and bring only a limited amount of cash with you.

Response: Be forthright: "I dislike talking about money, but I can't treat you every single time. I have to watch what I spend, too. I'll pay tonight, but we have to have an agreement in the future. We'll split checks from now on."

Alert: The fact that your friend never has cash or is maxed out on her credit cards is not your problem. She's been forewarned and will be ready for your *no*.

⬤ *The Scenario*

"I'm coming to town for a week, same week as last year. Can I stay with you?"

What's going on here: It's beginning to feel like you run a bed-and-breakfast for everyone who visits your city. You enjoy houseguests for short periods, occasionally, but this particular friend has worn out her welcome. She's been staying with you a week at a time for six years and has become, on top of being a world-class moocher, an in-your-face bore. She reports the minutia of each day's events. A few days you can handle, but seven has become grating. Years ago you moved her out of your inner circle; act on that decision. Let someone else take her in.

Response: "That's not going to be convenient."

Alert: Don't feel guilty when ending a freeloader's run, especially when it's been a long one. When she's worn out her welcome, you have every right to reclaim your home—and chances are she'll focus on finding hospitality elsewhere and not on the fact that she can't stay with you.

● *The Scenario*

"Dinner on Tuesday? Just us and a few friends."

What's going on here: Who are the others? Some friends invite people arbitrarily, paying no heed to how cohesive the group may be. Inadvertently you may be dining with friends of friends you don't like.

Response: "Who else is coming?"

Alert: When you don't get the whole story, probe for more or don't take the chance—skip that dinner or party.

You're Invited

It's affirming to be popular, to be included, to be swamped with invitations—to weddings, bar and bat mitzvahs, baby showers, and new house and dinner parties—to be together with the gang. And during the season to be jolly, you could be inundated with people to see and places to go. Even if you want to attend everything you're on the guest list for, it may not be possible.

It's never easy to tell someone you can't attend his son's graduation luncheon or her mother's birthday bash when that event is of utmost importance to the host. In the world of invitations, be they for pivotal occasions or casual dinners, here are predicaments and approaches you can try to ensure you accept only invitations that are a top priority to *you*.

⬤ The Scenario

"Can we get together New Year's Eve?"

What's going on here: New Year's Eve carries a sense of urgency, a command performance—one during which you're supposed to be jolly and entertaining even if you don't feel like it. The pressure to celebrate is enormous and can leave you feeling confused about with whom you want to party or if you want to party at all.

Response: "No, we're staying home this year." Or, "It's too early to know what we want to do."

Alert: How you decide to celebrate a holiday needs no explanation.

⬤ The Scenario

The invitation arrives: New Year's Day party, noon to 3:00 P.M.

What's going on here: You were looking forward to sleeping until noon and/or cleaning up your house from your own New Year's Eve soiree. If you need the time to recharge, take it so you can start off the New Year calm and rested. However, if that feeling of missing out creeps up on you— "everyone" will be there—but you don't want to go to a big party, invite a few friends for a casual celebration that is more your style.

Response: Check off the "no" box or call to say, "Sorry, we can't make it, but thank you for including us."

Alert: There will be plenty of opportunities to see friends throughout the year.

The Scenario

"We're having our annual Derby Day party. We're expecting you."

What's going on here: You hate going; horse racing holds no fascination for you. You'd rather clean a closet or read a book, but you've gone every year and you're a little worried about how backing out all of a sudden will be perceived. You worry your friends are very sensitive and will be insulted if you don't go. You can't say you're busy, because you knew the invitation was coming; it comes every year—and with it that dreaded sense of obligation.

Response: "I want to be with everyone, but I can seriously live without the Derby. Thank you, but I'm passing."

Alert: Beware of people who make assumptions or are so self-confident that they back you into a corner. You're entitled to your preferences and to act on them.

The Scenario

"Will you hold the 21st and the 28th open for dinner with us? We may have plans for one of those Saturdays, but I'm not sure which one."

What's going on here: At the moment you have nothing on your calendar for either Saturday, so you have no reason not to say, "Will do." What you really want to know is why these people can't commit to one date or the other. Might they be waiting to see if something better comes along while they keep you in limbo?

Response: "No, we can't tie up two weekends. Let's decide right now."

Alert: If friends waffle about dates or make hold-the-date requests often, begin to question how high you are on their priority list.

The Scenario

"Bring salad, I've got everything else covered."

What's going on here: Kelley calls you at home after work to invite you to a small dinner party at her place over the weekend. You're dog-tired and two things flash through your mind: no way do I want to be in charge of the salad and I detest washing lettuce. When you're tired, your resistance is low and you're apt to agree. What you should think is what can you offer that doesn't take time to prepare?

Response: "No, not salad. I'll bring wine."

Alert: Others have the most success eliciting a yes when your defenses are down from a tiring or a stressful day.

The Scenario

"We're planning a surprise party for Jake. Will you come?"

What's going on here: You're not close to Jake, maybe you don't like Jake. You could be shocked that you're even on the invitation list because you and Jake had a major falling out ages ago and are not speaking. The person contacting you has no idea of your relationship with Jake.

Response: A straightforward, "No, thank you, wish I could join you" will get you out of a potentially awkward situation. Don't offer explanations about the difficulties you and Jake have had.

Alert: The person calling has many more people to contact and probably doesn't care how you feel about Jake or how he feels about you.

○ *The Scenario*

"I'll be in Chicago for a few days, so we will have lots of time to catch up."

What's going on here: You want to see your friend, but you know she expects you to clear your calendar for her. She's possessive and on the high end of the self-centeredness scale. If you don't have every minute when you're not at work to devote to her, she plays the guilt card by saying, "Oh, I thought you'd be excited to see me."

Response: "That week is really crammed with dates. I won't be able to be with you full-time, but we'll still see each other."

Alert: Don't stop your busy life and allow a friend to monopolize it during an occasional visit. Include her in plans when you can. She'll find something to do when you're not available.

Out and About: Social Graces

Learn to be protective of your time—it's a valuable thing that you have in limited supply. When you divvy up your free time between too many people and obligations, you don't have any left over to say yes to yourself and what you want or know is good for you.

While it's impressive to be socially gracious, available, and adaptable, strategic nos preserve energy and help you avoid social burnout. Doing less for others frees you up to be a better friend, partner, parent, or employee because you are able to give more attention to what you choose to do instead of racing from chore to chore, commitment to commitment.

◐ *The Scenario*

"The Goodmans just had a baby. Can you make a meal and bring it over sometime this week?"

What's going on here: Your church or religious group expects its members to provide meals for people who have had a significant event in their lives—a new baby, an illness, a death. Helping now and again makes you feel you are giving back and making a contribution. Even if you wanted to cook for the Goodmans, however, right now you don't have time to shop for the ingredients, prepare a meal, and deliver it.

Response: "Can't this week, but try me another time. I always want to help out when I can."

Alert: Don't overextend yourself or volunteering will become a chore that you won't ever feel like doing.

◯ *The Scenario*

"We can clean and organize this dump in no time if we each take a room. You can start in the kitchen."

What's going on here: You and a few friends rented a run-down cottage house for the summer. It needs elbow grease on everyone's part. One of the gals elected herself foreman; she barks orders while the rest of you scrub. She's over-the-top bossy.

Response: "No. I think doing it my way will be more equitable and efficient. Let's try it."

Alert: People who take charge expect you to comply. Challenge them.

◯ *The Scenario*

Plans were made. You're in the car and on your way. Only then does your friend say, "Can we stop at Sal's on our way back? I'll run in; it will only take a sec."

What's going on here: Your friend throws her all too-familiar curveball once she has you captive. She thinks she can add extra stops at a shoe store, a grocery, another friend's house, wherever, but she never tells or asks you if you have the time or if you object until you are in her car. If you don't say something, you know that you will simmer the entire time you're together.

Response: "No, I have to be back by six. We can't do anything else or we'll get back too late for my sitter (an appointment, to start dinner)."

Alert: Listen for the "one more thing" ruse and don't allow it when it irritates you or messes up other plans you might have.

◯ *The Scenario*

"If we go to the jazz festival this weekend, I'll go anywhere you want to go next weekend. Deal?"

What's going on here: Enticing because you know just what you want to do next time, but if you made similar deals with this friend in the past and he doesn't hold up his end of the bargain, then think again.

Response: "No deal."

Alert: Be wary of friends who barter for your time; everyone may not be as good to his word as you are.

◯ The Scenario

"I'm taking my car up to my brother's so he can use it while we're away next week. Can I borrow Alex for a few hours on Saturday to follow me and bring me back?"

What's going on here: Friends regularly ask permission to "borrow" your partner, be it to help move a couch, fix their garage doors, find a leak, or whatever. He's strong, handy, and agreeable. You know it's over an hour and a half drive one way to her brother's house. He'll be gone four or five hours minimum.

Response: "I really need Alex around on Saturday." You could add the truth: my parents are visiting; to hang the blinds; to take our pet to the vet; to babysit while I have a birthday lunch with my sister.

Alert: Don't be too quick to lend your best helper when you may need him yourself.

◯ The Scenario

"The craft show opens Friday night. I'll meet you there after work."

What's going on here: Dictatorial people are hard to refuse. They know what they want and when they want it and are not concerned if you are inconvenienced. And, not surprisingly, whatever it is almost always makes their life far easier than it makes yours. You want to attend, but if you say yes to Friday night, you'll be driving miles in rush hour traffic, and that doesn't make sense. Present an alternative that suits you better.

Response: "Friday is not good for me. Let's go Saturday morning."

Alert: To make your life less difficult, consider what is most manageable for you first. People who make the best arrangements for themselves are the ones who know what they want and say no to be sure they get it.

● *The Scenario*

You get an e-mail, "Can we meet?"

What's going on here: You've searched through hundreds of dating service entries and at last found a potential date. You've seen his picture and he's more than passable. You've exchanged a steady stream of e-mails, and now he wants a face-to-face. And yes, you led him on a bit in a few e-mails, but a couple things he wrote set off your inner alarm.

Response: "No, I don't think it's a good idea." Explain nothing in your e-mail.

Alert: Don't worry about hurting the feelings of a "friend" you don't really know. Trust your instincts, save your time. Click on the next photo.

The Scenario

"Check out the guy with the blond hair over by the bar; he's adorable and looking right at you—an invitation if I ever saw one. Go talk to him."

What's going on here: Your friends coax you; they resort to name-calling, referring to you as a coward and a wimp. They are on your case and wearing you down. You think you should start a conversation with the guy just to shut them up.

Response: "If he wants to talk to me, he knows where I am."

Alert: Don't be goaded into doing things that you feel are dangerous, compromise who you are, or that you'll dislike yourself for doing.

The Scenario

"You have such good handwriting. Will you address the invitations?"

What's going on here: Your handwriting is clear and your letters angle neatly in one direction, but it's neither calligraphy nor fancy enough for the royal family. Is your friend's handwriting so terrible? Or are you being asked because your friend doesn't want to be bothered?

Response: "My handwriting is no better than yours. (Chuckle when you add:) Besides, you can just print them out on your computer."

Alert: If you think there's the slightest chance you'll be miserable while performing the task say no right away. You can change your mind later.

⬤ The Scenario

"We're thinking about hosting a going-away party for the Smiths. I don't know when I'll find the time to pull it together."

What's going on here: You know the person speaking well, and she is clearly on a fishing expedition to see if you take the bait. Being the good soul you are, it's a perfect opportunity to say that you'll help—and just as good an opportunity to keep your mouth shut. You like the Smiths and a party is the ideal send-off.

Response: "I don't have time to organize it either."

Alert: Don't rush in to be in charge. The party will be arranged eventually and you will get to participate.

⬤ The Scenario

"We'll meet at your apartment at seven and leave from there."

What's going on here: You know this group. Once they get to your place, they hunker down with chips and drinks and don't want to go out. By midnight your neighbor's hand will hurt from banging on the wall to quiet the din. Around two, you, the cleanup crew of one, start picking chips out of the cracks in the sofa and scrubbing beer stains off the rug.

Response: "No. Let's decide where we want to go and meet there."

Alert: When you know the drill, don't let history repeat itself.

◯ *The Scenario*

"I signed us up for the ski trip for the weekend of the 24th. Great idea, isn't it?"

What's going on here: Most of us have friends who micromanage (or try to) other people's lives and, when given the room, ours. Micromanagers possess finely honed skills to rope you in so subtly that you hardly realize what's happened. Even if you've been agreeing to a friend's directives for a very long time, you can get free.

Response: "No, I know you may think I'm a lousy friend, but I don't want to go. Count me out." Or, "I made other plans for the 24th, please take me off the list."

Alert: People who try to control others don't anticipate no for an answer. Refuse once or twice and they will ask before they obligate you again without your permission.

◯ *The Scenario*

"Can I be your fourth for the front nine holes?"

What's going on here: He's a nice enough guy off the golf course, but on it, he's a known cheater. Golfers who shave a stroke here and there make your blood boil. Isn't golf supposed to be relaxing, a game to enjoy with friends? Keep that in mind when you tell the cheat that he's not really welcome to play with your group.

Response: "I think Ted is our fourth; we play together all the time." Or, "We're waiting for Ted."

Alert: To avoid playing a round with golfers who cheat, slow down your game. For those who are loudmouths out on the course, arrange your foursomes before you get to the course.

◯ *The Scenario*

"We found you the perfect guy. Dinner at our place. Judd and I will be there to make the introduction easy and keep the conversation moving."

What's going on here: You've had more blind dates than you care to recall, none of them good, particularly the six your friends Ashley and Judd arranged. They truly care about you and have your best interests at heart, but they don't seem to understand what you're looking for. They believe they are doing you a favor. You, on the other hand, already know the tiresome routine: another awkward, uncomfortable evening that won't end soon enough, that's a complete waste of your time. Why subject yourself to such torture?

Response: "No, thank you. It's sweet of you to worry about me, but I'm taking a break from blind dates."

Alert: Because people care about you doesn't mean they understand what you want in a partner. Most likely good friends will not reject you as a friend because you turn down their blind date find. They'll actually keep looking.

The Scenario

"The members need to be alerted to the time change for the next meeting. Will you send e-mails to everyone?"

What's going on here: Why me? There are six other people in the room who can do it. For sure, someone's e-mail address has changed and the e-mail will bounce back. You'll have to track down the new one with a phone call. All this takes time.

Response: "No, can someone else please handle the e-mails?"

Alert: Dodging is more than an acceptable solution for overload.

The Scenario

"Are you going to John Johnson's funeral?"

What's going on here: We all want to do the right thing, but whoever is asking is not necessarily trying to make you feel guilty. He may be trying to decide what to do based on what you plan.

Response: "No. I didn't know him very well and I don't know anyone in his family." Or, "I'll stop by the house, but I'm not going to the funeral."

Alert: Funerals are not must-attend events unless you are among the deceased's close friends or in the family circle. You don't have to go to a funeral because someone asks you if you'll be there, nor should you feel compelled to do so.

◯ The Scenario

"Will you speak at George's funeral?"

What's going on here: It's an honor to be asked, but you have your doubts about standing up in front of a large group on this sad occasion. You're not sure you can or want to eulogize George, but how can you refuse?

Response: "No. I don't think I'm the right person; I'd be too emotional." Or, "I'm deeply moved that you asked me, but I didn't know him well enough." Or, "I can't speak to large groups." Or, "Have you asked Juan or Elise? They would be wonderful."

Alert: If you tense on hearing the request, *no* is the only answer that will spare you the stress you will surely feel in the days before and on the day of your eulogy and the burial.

◯ *The Scenario*

"Let's go to Andre's Continental for dinner?"

What's going on here: Andre's is one of the most expensive restaurants in the area, and you don't want to spend the money—or really can't afford to. Face it, you won't enjoy one bite because the price will be all you can think about. On the other hand, your style is to be obliging and you don't want to appear cheap.

Response: "No, let's go somewhere less expensive."

Alert: Accept that you can't afford what your friend can and enjoy the meal and the company at a more moderately priced establishment. People are not mind readers. No one knows that you object unless you say so.

◯ *The Scenario*

"This will be the best vacation weekend the four of us ever took. Here's the itinerary."

What's going on here: You've traveled with these friends many times—they present the plan as a fait accompli, and you go. Your friends don't like their choices questioned, and they always think their selections are ideal. They're fairly inflexible, so you worry about hurting their feelings or insulting them. Once you're wherever you're going, you're sorry you weren't more involved in the planning.

Response: "No. I want to look at the stops and hotels you've selected before we send a deposit. I heard about some unusual sights we might want to see."

Alert: Although a friend invested time to make the plans, it's your holiday and money, too. You can offer your input and nix those parts you don't like with a free conscience.

The Scenario

"You have to have the Super Bowl party. You've had that party for years. It's tradition."

What's going on here: For what seems like a decade your friends have gathered at your house to scream at the television set, drink your booze, and eat your food. The mess they leave behind is, well, a mess. Your enthusiasm has been on the wane for a long time, but you haven't wanted to disappoint your friends. You have put on your hostess face and smiled, wishing the fourth quarter would end. Not anymore.

Response: "No, I'm not hosting Super Bowl this year."

Alert: Bowing out and breaking a long-standing tradition will force someone else to take over, if he or she feels strongly enough about its preservation.

The Scenario

"What do you mean, you're not coming to the picnic? Of course you are."

What's going on here: Your friend loves picnics, and if she thought about it, she would remember that you don't. You can't be in the sun, don't like sand in your sandwich or pine needles in your potato salad. She's imposing her will on you. Why care if she thinks you're the proverbial stick-in-the-mud? You'll be in an air-conditioned room relaxing over your meal and using the time to catch up on reading or bill paying.

Response: "No, I don't eat outdoors, you know that."

Alert: Don't be bullied into being somewhere you don't want to be—in this instance, swatting flies and fending off mosquitoes. The itching isn't worth it.

● *The Scenario*

"Pick us up and we'll drive together?"

What's going on here: Picking up your friends may mean hiring the babysitter half an hour earlier and having her stay that much later, having to be ready sooner than you wanted, or driving out of your way.

Response: "No. That's not going to work for us tonight." Or, "We'd love to drive together, but it's inconvenient tonight. We'll meet you there" (unless they offer to pick you up).

Alert: Time is a precious commodity, and yours is as valuable as someone else's.

◯ *The Scenario*

"We're holding a one-day garage sale in two weeks. Will you help me set up and keep me company?"

What's going on here: You're wanted—and needed—for your keen ability to organize as well as for your companionship. Your friend will have you at her house days in advance pricing, setting up card tables, and telling her what she needs to do in the way of advertising. You'll be enlisted to post signs and make lunch. For you, the one-day garage sale could consume three or four days, or more.

Response: "I have all day Friday to get you ready, but I won't be there on sale day."

Alert: Be discerning in how you offer your time. Do what you can to have the event run smoothly, but only in the hours you allot.

◯ *The Scenario*

"I'll meet you at six to grab a bite to eat before the concert."

What's going on here: You said yes to the concert, but you planned on going home first, taking a shower, and saving money by eating the leftovers in your refrigerator.

Response: "I'll meet you at the concert. I'm going home first to unwind."

Alert: When you make arrangements, be clear so there's no room for misunderstanding or crossed wires.

◯ *The Scenario*

"We're set for the next two weekends. Friday we're going to Paul's party; Saturday we'll watch the race, then have dinner with Cliff and Joan; and Sunday we'll visit my sister to see the new baby. On the following weekend, we're going to Larry and Isabelle's. We are busy, aren't we?"

What's going on here: Your friend keeps you so booked, you have little time to be with other friends. When someone runs your life or tries to, it feels as if you're a pawn, or worse, as if he or she owns you. He masterminds what you do and when you do it and up until now, you've gone along with the program. It took a while to recognize the pattern and control he had over you, and it will persist unless you derail him.

Response: "That's a lot of planning and little asking. I can't do all that. I need some time to myself and to see other friends."

Alert: When you want your time back, you first have to recognize someone is monopolizing it before you can reclaim it.

◯ *The Scenario*

"We've waited this long, let's give Mary Kay another five minutes."

What's going on here: Mary Kay is one of those people who can be counted on to be late. Even when you build a cushion into a meeting time, it's never long enough. You can be accommodating to a point, but when someone's tardiness eats into your time, makes you nervous, or ruins your fun, it's time to stop tolerating the brash inconsideration. Apparently, Mary Kay doesn't respect or value your time. And by being late, she's controlling you.

Response: "No. I'm not waiting anymore."

Alert: Don't allow others to disrespect or abuse your time.

⬤ The Scenario

"Will you pick the restaurant for Saturday night?"

What's going on here: Your friends want to leave the dining decision up to you. That would be fine if every time you chose a restaurant they didn't find fault with the food, the service, the prices, the ambiance, or the noise level. While there's a lot to like about this couple, dining with them has become tedious. Have your answer ready.

Response: "No, thanks. You choose; you know what we like."

Alert: Think about the possible fallout from your choice. With impossible-to-please friends, bow out so you don't have to listen to them complain.

⬤ The Scenario

"There's a four o'clock showing of the movie I've been dying to see. How about I pick you up at three-thirty?"

What's going on here: Your friend calls with her movie picks fairly regularly. Since you don't keep up with the new releases, you usually go along with her choices. But after seeing so many bad movies, this time you're armed with the information you need.

Response: "No, I don't want to see that movie. Let's see the new comedy that the critics are raving about. I'll find out what time it starts and call you back."

Alert: When you know what you want, you may find that your friends are willing to follow your lead.

In the Neighborhood

The close proximity or essential give-and-take between friends and neighbors with children can become excessive and develop into dependent relationships. These relationships are open turf for a friend or neighbor taking advantage of your willingness to be there for her and assume responsibilities that could be allocated more evenly if you say no.

Putting off refusals is the same as having threatening storm clouds over your head. Procrastination adds extra stress to the relationship that doesn't have to be there. Firmly rejecting a request at the onset permits everyone to carry on. When you say no, the friend or neighbor moves on to ask someone else. She wants her own needs satisfied or her situation rectified and cares little who comes to her rescue.

○ The Scenario

"Can you drive carpool for me?"

What's going on here: The scheduled driver offers no hint of a possible emergency or suggestion that you would be doing her a favor—and she's done this before. It's not your day to chauffeur so you made a doctor's appointment (or scheduled a manicure). If you don't drive, you're concerned that your own child and your friend's will miss the soccer game. Don't be so sure. It is not your responsibility to see that these children get to *every* soccer game. When you say no, in all likelihood, the other parent will find a way to get her child and yours to the game.

Response: "No, I have plans."

Alert: If you willingly fill in this time, move yourself to the "sucker" category and count on being asked with great regularity.

○ The Scenario

"Will you watch my child for an hour on Thursday afternoon?"

What's going on here: This isn't the first time your friend has asked. What's really irksome is that her idea of an hour is quite protracted. She'll call to tell you she's stuck and apologize profusely—or she doesn't bother to call and you're stuck playing games and watching for her car.

Response: "No, I can't on Thursday."

Alert: Watch for patterns of behavior in others that leave you frustrated and at times furious.

The Scenario

"I know I said I would be in charge of the July Fourth street party this year, but would you print up the announcement flyer?"

What's going on here: It's that time of year and someone has to organize the neighbors or the party won't happen. You don't want to let them down, but you've run it for the past five years. It's been a huge success because of your organizational skills and follow-through. Printing the flyers is a small request; you could do it.

Response: "No, I'll give you the announcement from last year to copy."

Alert: You'll be surprised at how efficiently a job gets done without you. Give up control—you've earned it; neighborhood parties, fund-raisers, and other events can be successful without your overseeing them.

The Scenario

"I'm running late, again. I'm so sorry. Can you feed my kids and let them nap with yours?"

What's going on here: This friend is pushing her luck. You've had her children playing with yours since first thing this morning. It seems the children are always at your house, hardly ever at hers. And your children are too excited to fall asleep when their playmates are visiting.

Response: "No. Please come for them as soon as you can. I'll give them lunch, but they can't nap here today."

Alert: When the sharing of child responsibilities isn't reciprocal, start asking for equal time instead of feeling used.

The Scenario

Your friend complains about her child's science fair assignment. "I'm practically illiterate when it comes to that stuff," she says. "Any ideas?"

What's going on here: Whether or not she knows you excelled in the sciences and can think of twelve possible projects for her child and you to do together, unless you really want to tie up your Saturday and maybe Sunday, too, listen, but refrain from saying, "I'd be glad to help her."

Response: You may want to commiserate, "Don't teachers realize parents wind up doing 90 percent of the projects?" but then say, "I'll give your daughter a few suggestions, but I can't work on them with her this weekend."

Alert: With some people, listening to them vent is all you need do. You are still a good friend without sharing your talents with your friend's children. It's enough that you are called on to craft magnificent solar systems and working rockets for your own offspring.

◯ *The Scenario*

Mrs. Locke, your elderly neighbor, lives alone and has just recovered from surgery. She calls to ask if you would buy a birthday card for her to send to her son.

What's going on here: Several months ago you told her son, who lives across the country, not to worry—you would do his mother's shopping, take care of her garbage and recycling, and check on her until she was back on her feet completely. You did that and more—you cooked and brought her meals and drove her on errands long after she was able to drive again and manage her day-to-day needs herself.

Response: "Mrs. Locke, I can't get to the card store today. Why don't you pick up a card tomorrow when you're out shopping?"

Alert: When an emergency passes, when the person you are assisting can and should be independent again, you are doing her a disservice by prolonging the dependency. It's time to put *no* into action.

◯ *The Scenario*

"Will you request Michael for the team you're coaching this season?"

What's going on here: Your friend asks you to use your influence as a coach with the powers that make up the town's sports teams.

Response: "Michael's so good, he will do well on any team. He's got real potential."

Alert: You've taken an approach that will move your friend's focus back where it should be: on her son's athletic prowess. Without saying so, you've refused and not been forced to make a request that's potentially awkward.

The Scenario

"Kent is an awful athlete. We recognize that, but he'll be heart-broken if he's not on your team and with your son. Can you pull some strings to make sure they're together?"

What's going on here: When the boys were younger and learning the game, the makeup of the team wasn't so impor-tant. With the competition fierce in your son's age group, who's on what team takes on new significance. You're the coach and frankly, you want the strongest players on your team. Kent is not one of them. He is a great kid and one of your son's closest friends.

Response: "I can't make any promises. When they make up teams, they try to even them out so they're competitive."

Alert: Be vague when necessary. Don't commit yourself or say you will try when you can't or won't.

The Scenario

"Will you write a recommendation to your college for my son/daughter?"

What's going on here: You've been an interviewer for your alma mater for years, and you know your friend's child is not a candidate the college seeks. Your friend believes your recommendation counts, that it will wow admissions and get her child into college.

Response: "My letter won't help."

Alert: Implying that you don't have much clout gives your friend a strong hint that you aren't enthusiastic about recommending his child. You've said no indirectly and haven't compromised your integrity with the college, so you can write recommendations in the future.

The Scenario

"Hope you don't mind, but they're coming to cut down our dead tree at eight on Saturday morning."

What's going on here: Your neighbor would not be asking if he were sure the time was okay. He knows you sleep late on Saturday. Most people say, "Fine. Thanks for letting me know," then fume about being awakened so early.

Response: "That's too early. Ask them to start at nine."

Alert: Instead of accepting what people tell you, ask for a change that accommodates you.

The Scenario

"Dinner. Saturday night?" your neighbor chirps brightly.

What's going on here: Nice gesture. Friendly, but boring, couple. Other than the children who play together, you have nothing in common. Confine your socializing with the gracious couple to neighborhood picnics, conversations across the yard, and play date arrangements.

Response: "Thanks, but we can't make it," polite, short, and sweet. Lengthy explanations lead to complicated stories and potentially troubling entanglements. You don't want to have to sit in a darkened house, crawling under the windows to get to another room on Saturday night because you said you were going out.

Alert: You can be warm and neighborly and dispense goodwill without sharing meals and becoming intimate.

The Scenario

A child from the neighborhood dressed in her Girl Scout uniform rings your doorbell. "Hi, Mrs. D'Angelo, I'm selling cookies for my troop. Will you buy some?" Her mother stands in the background watching your reaction.

What's going on here: The last things on your must-buy list are cookies or candy or another magazine subscription, but you also want to be neighborly.

Response: "I placed an order with my niece." You could say, "I can't do it now (or today)" and hope she forgets to stop by another day.

Alert: It's nearly impossible to refuse a child you know. However, you can say no to children you don't know and should turn away anyone raising money for causes that are unfamiliar or could be shams.

◯ The Scenario

"We need two hundred names on this petition," a neighbor says, and then he rambles on about what a good thing the petition is for the community and how everyone is signing. *"Please, sign here,"* he adds, thrusting the pad into your hand.

What's going on here: You're unclear on the issue or the group behind it. You don't know how the petition will be used and don't like to sign unless you believe in the cause 100 percent. Your neighbor is persistent.

Response: "I don't put my name on anything I haven't read thoroughly. Leave me a copy; I can't read it now."

Alert: Don't sign petitions of any type unless you understand their purpose and how they will be used.

◯ The Scenario

"You got your planting done before noon. I'm impressed. Can you help me get these last few plants in my garden before it rains?"

What's going on here: You're a high-energy person with lots to spare after a full morning of physical labor, and your neighbors, sister, mother, aunt, and uncle know it.

Response: "I'm gardened out."

Alert: Most high-energy people think they can do more than they actually can. Like caving in and agreeing when you're tired and your defenses are down, you are just as likely to say yes during your peak energy periods. When you're in high gear, don't announce that you'll be right over to do someone else's chores. Save the extra energy for yourself. When you're feeling at the top of your game, be cautious about what you agree to do so you're not sorry when you have to help. It's perfectly acceptable to do nothing sometimes.

The Scenario

"Will you let the deliverymen into my house sometime between noon and five? You work from home; you'll be around."

What's going on here: In spite of the incredible number of people who conduct business from their homes, the common belief is that those with home offices are not busy and have the time to oblige their neighbors, friends, and family.

Response: "I'll be waiting for an important call." Or, "I have to run some business errands." Or, "I have a conference call scheduled." Or, "I'm on deadline." In short, tell the neighbor it's impossible for you to watch for deliverymen for five hours on a workday. (It's disruptive enough when you have to do it for yourself.)

Alert: To stop people from thinking you spend Monday to Friday knitting and baking, be unavailable to chat in the middle of the day. Get a separate office phone line and give the number to business associates only, or add caller ID to your phone service and answer only work-related calls.

2

All in the Family

Life, in a word, is hectic. Jobs, schedules, commitments, and demands come at you from all directions and swallow whole days and weeks. The requests are so prevalent it can be nearly impossible to decide whose you want to meet. At times you can find yourself borderline frantic trying to get everything accomplished. While it's feasible to dismiss a friend to make life less chaotic, it's harder to reduce the family circle. You can't cut off one relative without affecting other relationships within the family.

Similarly, family needs are among the most difficult to satisfy because one seemingly innocuous *no* can ignite a family feud or division that lasts for months, years, or a lifetime. When one unforgiving family member takes offense at your *no*, the effects dribble down to other relatives. In short, you can have a disturbing familial mess.

Relatives are the people you love most dearly and conversely are the ones who infuriate you with their incessant requests. For complex reasons that have developed over the years, you don't want to disappoint them or be faced with their disdain. To make matters worse, you've convinced yourself that you're supposed to be there for them, that it's your job to help solve their problems and keep the peace. If you've fallen into the confining role of always being there for family, you are going to have to adjust your thinking—and practice diligently to free yourself from being the family do-it-all.

When you say yes continually to others, you say no to yourself and relegate yourself to second position or fourth or last. You tell yourself and your family that you are not important, that they come first.

Tightening Your Boundaries

As enjoyable as relatives can be, there are times they invade your privacy, ask the outrageous, or make demands that as a busy adult you can't meet. But because of the history and closeness, saying no to them seems impossible. And to make it even harder, relatives are much more likely to know your weaknesses, and when they hone in on one your resistance vanishes.

Are you the go-to person in your family? Within the family your reputation for diligence precedes you, and you've convinced yourself that things don't get done unless you do them. You buy the gifts, send the flowers, visit the hospital, grocery shop with your great aunt, and handle any and all emergencies. Don't you often think you're the only dependable grown-up in the family? The trouble is, your whole family thinks that way, too. Where is your sister when you need her? Why doesn't your brother ask what he can do?

Rebuilding, fortifying, and defending your boundaries will greatly reduce the frustration of never having enough time and relieve the anger you feel toward those whose demands chip away at your time.

It's time to get tough so you don't give your life over to your family's bidding in the guise of being a "good" person who is nothing more than the family lackey. You can stay in your family's good graces *and* still turn them down.

As you will see from the following family scenarios, *no* is the cornerstone of self-respect and your gateway to being able to concentrate on what makes you feel better and more in command of your life.

If you truly are to be your own person, you have to practice self-protection, and that means sometimes you have to say no to those you love.

◯ *The Scenario*

"We're having girls' night out with Mom next Friday. You'll join us, won't you?"

What's going on here: Mother and daughters have been having dinner and a movie night together once a year for most of your adult life, and almost all those evenings have been excruciating experiences for you. Your sisters are only too happy to tell you what you are doing wrong with your life, your makeup, and in your job. You have told them that this bothers you, but their behavior hasn't changed. You don't want to be the one who ruins the tradition, and every year you think this night will be different and they won't attack you, but they do.

Response: "I can't be there." (You don't have to explain or give excuses because you are a grown-up.)

Alert: Wishful thinking will not prevent your siblings and mother from hurting your feelings or insulting you. They can't help themselves. They have been behaving this way so long that they are not apt to stop now. Stay away.

◯ *The Scenario*

Your Uncle Ned asks, "Let's go to Disney World, my treat. Should I get tickets for the children's spring break or summer vacation?"

What's going on here: He's trying to buy your loyalty and love. It's a generous and almost irresistible gift, but one that you will pay for many times over. For starters, you will have to be pleasant to him, his airhead wife, and his impossible children the whole time you're together. He will dictate what rides to ride and what sights to see while boastfully reminding you what a great guy he is.

Response: "Thanks, Uncle Ned, but we're saving Disney World until the children are older."

Alert: You will be in Uncle Ned's debt and forced to suffer his superiority for longer than you can imagine. Before you accept, decide if the trip is worth the groveling you'll have to do.

● *The Scenario*

"My gifts never look as beautiful as yours. Will you wrap these presents for me?"

What's going on here: Your mother, aunt, sister, or other relative is making her "I'm incapable" appeal. You're the family's Martha Stewart of gift wrapping, which may or may not reflect your talent, but more to the point, if she can hoodwink you into doing her wrapping how much the better— for her.

Response: "No, your wrappings are fine" (or "more than adequate" or "very attractive").

Alert: Dispel the myth that you do anything or everything exceptionally well as quickly as you can.

The Scenario

"Will you organize the food for the family reunion?"

What's going on here: Planning food for ten or forty, even if you don't have to make it yourself, is a huge undertaking. The family thinks because you like to cook, you're the person to handle meals.

Response: "No. I'll be happy to arrange for all the lunches, but someone else has to take over the other meals."

Alert: Compromising and allocating is the fair solution for making you feel less burdened.

The Scenario

"Will you arrange the flowers for the table?"

What's going on here: You've agreed to prepare the main course and pick up Uncle Harold. If flowers are your thing, then ask someone else to cook the entrée or retrieve Uncle Harold.

Response: "No, I won't have time."

Alert: Remember that you don't have to do every single thing asked of you.

⬤ *The Scenario*

Aunt Judy is about to tell you—pound by pound—how she lost all the weight. "Darling, I have to tell you about a marvelous new weight loss regimen."

What's going on here: After trying a hundred different diets yourself, you're not going to get into it with Aunt Judy at a family party. With her svelte new figure, she's going to make you feel terrible (you're embarrassed by your still-chunky self anyway) and, more dangerous, convince you on the spot to test her new diet program. Doing so means investing dollars you don't have right now.

Response: "Aunt Judy, you look great, but I don't want to talk about diets today."

Alert: Avoid topics and stop conversations you know will make you feel bad by declaring them off-limits.

⬤ *The Scenario*

"When you shop for Kristin's graduation gift, would you pick something up from me?"

What's going on here: You're having a hard enough time figuring out what you will buy the graduate. Finding something for your sister to give is asking too much of your creative mind.

Response: "I don't know what we are giving her. You're on your own with this one."

Alert: Abandon the need to rescue everyone in the family who asks; leave them to solve their own small dilemmas.

The Scenario

"You're including your cousins in the party, aren't you? I always did."

What's going on here: Your relatives are getting older and you've taken over the responsibility for some of the celebratory gatherings, but your mother's or aunt's guest list is not the same as yours, nor does it have to be. You want to avoid a confrontation, so you shy away from telling them that you've taken people off the list. Say how you feel and you'll have a better time.

Response: "No, I am not inviting Scott and Marilyn. I don't enjoy them (they argue with my husband; I never liked them; I don't have enough space at the table)."

Alert: After the first party or two at your home, the family's expectations will change.

The Scenario

"You'll take the photos at your cousin's wedding, won't you?"

What's going on here: Could be your mother asking or your aunt, the bride's mother. Whoever has volunteered your artistic eye makes the assumption that you want this scary assignment. You're good, but you are not a professional photographer; you don't have a staff holding lights and a backup camera. You shoot pictures for fun and as an occasional gift. Think this one through: What if the batteries wear down just as the groom feeds your cousin the first piece of wedding cake? What if you shoot the last frame in the camera seconds before he toasts her? Nervous yet? When will you get to dance or chat? If you want to do something creative for your cousin, decorate the getaway car or write your own toast.

Response: "No. That's a responsibility I will not assume."

Alert: When the need for pitch-perfect performance is high and the responsibility weighty, advise the family to hire a "real" photographer or appropriate professional to do the required job.

◯ *The Scenario*

"Let's give Beth a baby shower together."

What's going on here: You wanted to give Cousin Beth a shower by yourself. She's more like a sister than a cousin. You believe a joint shower diminishes your role as her best and closest friend and doesn't tell Beth how important she is to you. Refusing another family member might set off a whole chain reaction within the family—but it might not. And, in the excitement of a new baby, your decision will likely become insignificant.

Response: "No, I really want to do this myself. I've been thinking about it since Beth got married. It's something I have to do. I hope you understand."

Alert: Once you've made it clear how meaningful hosting the event is to you, do what pleases you. The others can and will give their own shower(s) if they feel as compelled and committed as you do.

The Scenario

"The baby is due at the end of July. Will you stay with the children while I'm in the hospital?"

What's going on here: Staying with the older children may be what you do in your family when a newborn arrives. You feel obligated, but your responsibilities have changed since the last family baby was born: you have a job, or your children are older and must be driven to activities at crazy hours, or you are taking care of a sick relative—or you just don't want to.

Response: "I know I stayed with Lizzie when Ian was born, but it's impossible for me to do that now."

Alert: Even for major life events, give yourself permission to say no, especially if you've pitched in on other occasions. Someone else in the family will take over.

The Scenario

"I know it's short notice, but will you babysit for us over the weekend?"

What's going on here: Your sister, brother, niece, or other relative asks at the last minute. She does this regularly, and you usually save her. Because you babysit at a moment's notice, she'll be expecting you to do so this time. In her mind, you can be counted on to be there whenever she needs you. Unless they can't be helped, short-notice requests because of poor planning are inconsiderate.

Response: "I can't this weekend. I'm always delighted to have the children, but I have to have a bit of advance warning."

Alert: When people take advantage of you, the most serious repercussion is the irritation *you* feel for making yourself available to others 24/7.

⬤ The Scenario

"Will you paint a border in your niece's room? You're her godmother and it would delight her so."

What's going on here: Your sister or sister-in-law is asking you to spend a weekend or two handcrafting a special look in your godchild's room and playing on your special godmother-goddaughter bond to boot. She thinks if she reminds you that godmothers have distinct duties (not true) you'll be thrilled at the suggestion.

Response: "What a great idea. Let's wait until Alyssa is older and she and I will do it together." Or, "I'm flattered, but I don't have the time right now." Or, "I don't know where you got the idea that I was artistic enough for the job" (if true).

Alert: The guilt trip signal is flashing red. If you say no you will feel like the world's worst godmother—temporarily. If you agree, you will begin to resent your sister or sister-in-law for roping you into something you don't want to do.

● *The Scenario*

Your brother asks, "Can you keep the children busy this afternoon so I can put the final touches on the new playroom? It's almost done."

What's going on here: Another afternoon is about to evaporate. This morning you baked blueberry muffins with your niece and nephew to keep them out of your brother's hair. Last weekend, you took them bike riding and to watch hot air balloon races to give him time to lay the flooring. You adore your brother, but he's starting to sound like your mother, who had a never-ending list of things for you to do.

Response: "Give me a break. I need the afternoon to myself."

Alert: You don't have to comply with all requests to be appreciated, particularly when they are excessive. If you do, others in the family will catch on and try to snare chunks of your time.

● *The Scenario*

"I made a reservation at Old Mill Inn for Dad's birthday party. He loves it there. Will that be fine for you and Charles?"

What's going on here: Surprise, surprise: the restaurant is convenient for your sibling, but a major pain for you and Charles to get to. In most families there's one person who dictates (or tries to) where and when family milestone events are held. You're tired of feeling as if you have no say, but it's almost always easier to go along than face a battle. However, the pleasure you get from having it your way for a change is worth the effort.

Response: "It's time we went somewhere else. How about Little Italy?"

Alert: Suggesting an alternate location may yield a positive response from the whole family. Go for it next time you feel you're being railroaded.

⬤ *The Scenario*

"We want to relocate Uncle Eddie into an assisted living complex, but we don't know where to begin looking."

What's going on here: The questions are implied: What do you know about such facilities? Will you research on the Internet, call the insurance company, pick up some caregiving books, go visit some places? Your expertise is being sought, and it's your nature to volunteer helpful ideas and information.

Response: "It's foreign territory to me" (if it is). Or, "We had such bad experiences with my mom/dad/aunt/uncle, I'm afraid I'm no help" (if true). Recommend a person with experience or knowledge if possible.

Alert: Wait until you are asked for concrete information or assistance. Exercise self-restraint or you could be making the arrangements and settling Uncle Eddie alone.

⬤ The Scenario

"It's been months since Grandma died. Will you divide her belongings as you see fit and send us whatever? We just want a token that will remind us of Grandma."

What's going on here: You live the closest, so you've been elected to sort your grandmother's belongings and divide them among your siblings. You can pretty much count on one of your siblings being unhappy with how you divvy up Grandma's dishes and jewelry. They say they don't care, but they do. In the end, agreeing will be more painful than insisting you won't do it by yourself. Save heartache and bad feelings by saying . . .

Response: "I will not go through Grandma's things by myself. One of you will have to fly here and we'll do it together."

Alert: No matter how evenhandedly you think you handle the distribution, someone will feel cheated if you unilaterally make all the decisions.

⬤ The Scenario

"Can you help Dad pack up the basement on Saturday? My kids have soccer (baseball, football, tennis) tournaments (games, practice)."

What's going on here: Your "excuse" sibling is doing what she does best. If she isn't using her children to exempt her, she'll have a bridal shower or wedding to attend, a guest in from out of town, or be in the middle of a project she can't possibly stop to avoid helping her father—or you.

Response: "No, I can't be there Saturday. How about we both go over on Sunday?"

Alert: Answering a question with a question catches people unprepared with an excuse. Since you know you will help your father at some point, changing the schedule may lock in your sister.

The Scenario

"What do you mean, you're not going to Jill's gallery opening? She's worked for years to get a show of her photos, and you're not going to be there to support her? You have to go. What kind of person are you?"

What's going on here: Your sister, mother, father, aunt, or brother shouts and refuses to accept your *no*. Your reasons for not going could range from having something else scheduled to not caring about Jill or her photography, but you don't say this and you don't get into a screaming match. Stay as calm as you can to prevent the situation from escalating to the point of insults and your saying something you will be sorry for later.

Response: "It's not possible, and that's the way it is. I'll stop in to see Jill's show another time" (if you will).

Alert: When the pressure is on for you to relent, repeat to yourself, "I will not give in, I will not give in" to help you stick to your refusal.

◯ *The Scenario*

"I hate to ask you again, but could you send a check for the repairs on Mom's roof?"

What's going on here: Your sibling calls to ask you to foot the whole bill for the new roof, the new car, the airline tickets, a holiday gift. Your sibling has it in mind that you are the rich relative, a bottomless pit of money. Your parents and/or your siblings treat you as if you were their private banker. When it starts to feel as if they love your money more than they love you, it's time to stop supporting the family.

Response: "I can't do it alone. I'm strapped myself." Or, "My money's invested."

Alert: Don't boast about your financial windfalls or provide too many details of promotions that carry significant raises.

◯ *The Scenario*

Today's question from your sister is, "Any suggestions on how I can bring Jim back into my life?"

What's going on here: Every day she has a question or something she needs your help with: the kids won't do their homework, she can't figure out how to get both children to sports practice on different fields at the same time, she needs a job, the recipe doesn't taste as good as when you make it. She thinks she's the only one with problems, the only one with too much to do. She leans on you to pick up her pieces, to listen to her every tale of woe. She's always had a calamity in her life, and you've always come to her rescue in one way or another. Dealing with her problems has gotten old; it's time to stop.

Response: "No, I've got my own crises today."

Alert: Reduce the time you spend with or talk to high-maintenance relatives so you have emotional reserves for your own tasks and problems. With some people, no matter how much you do it's not enough.

◯ *The Scenario*

"It will be more fun if we shop together for Mom and Dad's gifts."

What's going on here: You and your sister have entirely different taste, and that fact hasn't changed since you were children: you lean toward the practical and she goes for the fanciful. Shopping together can only end in a disagreement about the right choices for Mom and Dad. You hesitate to give up control because you know you will dislike her selections. If you're wise, you'll turn the job over to her and gratefully go along with whatever she chooses as the joint gifts.

Response: "You go ahead. Just tell me what I owe you and I'll write you a check."

Alert: Relinquish control to get out of commitments you know will be problematic.

◯ The Scenario

"I love spending New Year's Eve with the family. We have such a good time. I'm making reservations for the four of you."

What's going on here: "We have such a good time" is a gross overstatement; you had an okay time at best. You enjoy your family, but your almost-teenage children want to celebrate with their friends, and frankly so do you.

Response: "Not this year. We already made other plans."

Alert: Nothing is etched in stone except epitaphs in cemeteries.

◯ The Scenario

"How about I take the children swimming so you can have the afternoon to yourself?"

What's going on here: Your heart skips a beat at your sister's (or mother's) offer. You need a break, but she's the last person on earth you would entrust with your children near water. She's easily distracted; you imagine her in her bathing suit chatting it up with someone she's just introduced herself to. She swivels her body away from the water to answer her new acquaintance's question while your darling children doggy paddle alone in the water.

Response: "That is so nice of you. Let's all go." Or, "Thanks, but not today."

Alert: It's no day off if you are going to worry yourself sick the entire time the children are in someone else's care. Saying no moves boundaries into your comfort zone.

Complicating Factors with Parents

Parents present the supreme challenge in the quest to mark your boundaries and be more of a *no* person. They, collectively, and granted maybe one less so than the other, spent their parenting careers getting you to obey them—to be polite and obedient, to do what they said when they said it. Over the years you have developed set patterns of reacting to your parents' requests. But times have changed. You are a grown-up with a life and perhaps a family of your own.

You no longer have to be the obedient, compliant child and will be much happier when you get out from under a parent's domineering or even just mildly annoying ways.

Few adult children set out to insult, hurt, or disregard their parents, but there may be many times when your parents, out of long-standing habit, continue to advise you, protect you, and think they know what's best. You may believe because it's your parent asking that saying yes is mandatory, that shaking your head no is unthinkable. Your yeses are expected, but frequently with parents you can anticipate situations and problems. In those cases, picture yourself saying no as a means to buttress your courage.

Saying no when you need to, even if your parents are not intrusive, will help validate your independence and force them to realize you deserve their respect.

◉ *The Scenario*

On the phone, your mother pleads, "Come by. I want to discuss something that I'd rather not talk about on the phone."

What's going on here: You cringe at the sound of her voice on the other end of the line. You have a mother who only counts in hour blocks. It takes her more than a minute to seal an envelope. If she gets you to stop in she will stall and talk to detain you for as long as she possibly can. For an instant, you flash back to all the times you were punished when you didn't do what she asked. Mothers are the hardest to say no to, but you can learn how to.

Response: "Not today, Mother, I simply can't."

Alert: Abandon any inclination to make excuses.

◯ The Scenario

"I haven't seen you in so long I forgot what you look like."

What's going on here: Ah, manipulation in its purest form. The ploy is designed to elicit your guilt, especially if you have been ignoring your parent because your life is too full. He or she is likely to be just as dismayed if you rush in and out as he will be if you don't stop at all.

Response: "No, I love you and want to be with you. Let's set a date."

Alert: You are entitled to a life that excludes parents and family some of the time. Make arrangements to visit when it works for you.

◯ The Scenario

Your husband answers the phone and says, "Honey, it's your mother. Can you talk?"

What's going on here: You spoke to your mother earlier in the day and you can tell your husband knows it by the roll of his eyes. She's so sensitive that she's going to be hurt if you don't pick up the phone.

Response: "Tell her I'll call back later."

Alert: You don't have to be available to your parent every single second. Whatever your mother has to say probably can wait.

The Scenario

"Do you mind if I bring Sandra with me when I come to visit next weekend?"

What's going on here: Sandra is your mother's best friend and constant sidekick since your parents' divorce. Sandra is supercritical and takes over your home the second she arrives. You rarely say no to your mother and are afraid to start now, but you don't want to be bothered by Sandra's meddling ways.

Response: "Mother, no, I prefer you came alone. We don't need Sandra with us whenever we're together. Let's just do a mother-daughter weekend."

Alert: Don't be afraid to ruffle a parent's feathers. She'll be flattered that you want to be with her one-on-one.

The Scenario

"I'm adding Aunt Becky and Uncle Al to the wedding guest list."

What's going on here: Aunt Becky is your mother's third cousin, and you haven't seen her or Uncle Al since you were three years old, nor do you care to see them on your wedding day. You may have to remind your mother that this is your wedding, not the one she wanted for herself or dreamed of for you. She might argue and tell you that she and your father are footing the bill, but you still don't have to invite people you barely know to a celebration that is purportedly for you. Stand firm; your mother will get the message.

Response: "No. I realize you don't want to hurt anyone's feelings, but we're trying to keep the wedding small. If we invite Aunt Becky, we have to invite her brothers and sisters, and on it goes. We'll be way over the number we agreed on. I'd be too nervous with all those people."

Alert: You probably spent your life trying to please your parents, but you have every right to edit the wedding guest list.

The Scenario

"What do you mean you're not asking your cousin to be in the bridal party? You grew up together."

What's going on here: You did, indeed, grow up together. You were forced to play with her when you didn't want to; you had to do whatever she wanted. Excluding family holiday celebrations, as you grew up you saw less and less of each other. By the teen years you tolerated your cousin, but had nothing in common. You'd feel like a hypocrite if she was in your wedding party, and it would mean having to leave out a dear friend.

Response: "I know how you feel, Mother, but I can't ask her. She's not part of my life anymore. We decided we only want our friends, and we're not changing our minds." In fact, you can add, "No one else in the family is in the bridal party other than the maid of honor and best man."

Alert: Be prepared for hard feelings and upset relatives, but that will be easier to face than a cousin you barely relate to walking down the aisle on your wedding day when it's not what you wanted.

◯ *The Scenario*

"We're going to pay for your honeymoon," your parents tell you. "When you're in Rome, will you stop for a short visit with your cousins?"

What's going on here: You may not want to go to Italy on your honeymoon, and if you do, you certainly don't want to be locked into a day with twice or three times removed cousins. And the person you're marrying may have a whole different idea on where you start your married life.

Response: "No, thank you. We've decided to go to Paris."

Alert: Don't allow parents to dictate your marital beginnings. You open up doors to their controlling your new life. Once opened, they are difficult to close.

◯ *The Scenario*

Your parents exclaim, "You're not moving into that apartment, are you?"

What's going on here: Many parents have a difficult time letting go of their children—their independent, self-supporting adult children. They will look for—and find—flaws galore with any choice: the neighborhood is too dangerous, the space is too small, not enough closets, too noisy, too isolated, too far from us.

Response: "Yes, I am. I love it."

Alert: Don't permit your parents to undermine your confidence. When you know what you want to do, make the decision and tell them after the fact.

◯ *The Scenario*

"These are the perfect dishes for you and Rob. If you don't buy them, your father and I will buy them for you."

What's going on here: You live with someone, you're married or about to marry, and your mother seems to forget that there are two of you making choices. She is not one of them, but from her statement it's clear she wants to be. She continues to see you as her little girl in whose life she plays the choreographer.

Response: "No, Rob and I selected a different pattern."

Alert: When you give more weight to your partner's and your own preferences than to your parents', it's much easier to say no to a parent.

⬤ *The Scenario*

"When was the last time you spoke to your brother? You should call him: it's important the two of you stay close," your mother instructs for the fifth time this week.

What's going on here: Why can't she tell your brother to phone you? She says she doesn't want to bother him; she says he's so busy; she says she doesn't want to talk to his wife, who usually answers the phone (none of which is your concern). She targets you because you do what she asks.

Response: "I'm not calling Barry again until he calls me."

Alert: Keeping ties strong takes more than one willing family member.

⬤ *The Scenario*

Your sister wants to know if you will call Dad to see if you can convince him to change his mind and join the family for dinner.

What's going on here: Your father and your brother-in-law have had a nasty verbal disagreement—a shouting match, in fact. You will only stir the pot and find yourself starting out to make peace and winding up embroiled in a dispute that had nothing to do with you in the first place.

Response: "I'm not going to be the intermediary."

Alert: Stay as far away as you can from family feuds that don't directly involve you—there'll be enough that do. Trying to be the peacemaker saps too much energy—and time.

◯ The Scenario

"I'm begging you to invite your sister and Gary."

What's going on here: A parent is trying to orchestrate your relationship with a sibling. Your sister and her partner are unreliable and inconsiderate; they arrive late enough to ruin a meal you've cooked or to make you late for an appointment, and they don't apologize. If a parent pleads, she knows that you've been tolerating your sister and brother-in-law's selfish behavior for a long time. Your parent is struggling to keep the family unit whole.

Response: "I'm not putting myself in that position again."

Alert: Enough already of being the good guy or good gal. You don't have to take indirect insults—relatives or not. Excluding the offenders may open their eyes to the reality that they can't ignore or disregard your feelings. It may be rough going for a while, but the discomfort will sort itself out in time.

◯ The Scenario

The inevitable tug of war begins when your mother announces, as she always does, "Thanksgiving dinner is Thursday at five o'clock." She neither acknowledges nor accepts excuses, nor will she move the dinnertime to accommodate spouses and their families. She's obstinate, but that shouldn't be news to you. She's refused your request to host Thanksgiving since you got married.

What's going on here: You want to serve Thanksgiving dinner at your house. You want to prove to yourself, your parents, and your friends that you can do it. Or maybe you want to sit at the head of the table, your table, on this important family holiday. You want to feel like a grown-up on Thanksgiving, but your mother doesn't seem to care how you feel.

Response: "No, Mother, Thanksgiving dinner this year is at my house at five o'clock."

Alert: It is always possible to change tradition. Although parents may balk initially, they generally adjust to the adult offspring's wishes as long as they are included.

The Scenario

"Can't you let him sit in the backseat? He's old enough, and we're only going a short distance," your mother tells you as you struggle to get your squirming three-year-old into his car seat.

Response: "No, Mother, he has to be buckled into his seat."

What's going on here: Your parent may be unaware that laws, safety precautions, and equipment have changed dramatically since she drove babies and toddlers. A gentle update may be all she needs.

Alert: No matter how controlling your mother, when it comes to your child's safety, you are in charge.

◯ The Scenario

"You're such good parents. When are you having another child?"

What's going on here: This question comes frequently from grandparents, friends, and surprisingly, from strangers in playgrounds, and can be particularly tedious if you have and are committed to raising an only child. Amazingly, other people seem to think they know what's good for you and your family.

Response: "We're not." And a curt reply at that should feel about right for those nervy enough to interfere, even if the question raises or reawakens doubts you may have.

Alert: Only you and your partner should be weighing in on family size decisions.

◯ The Scenario

"You're going to wait a year to start Will in kindergarten, aren't you?"

What's going on here: Your relative, be it your sister-in-law, aunt, mother, uncle, or cousin, is telling you what you should do without being asked. She's insinuating that your son is not mature enough to handle school and making a hard call all the more difficult.

Response: "We haven't decided what we're doing."

Alert: Family members seem to feel they have a right to offer opinions about your children. Ignore them or you will be in continuous turmoil about your parenting choices.

● The Scenario

"You need to buy stock with the money you inherited from your grandmother. Let me help you decide."

What's going on here: Your grandmother left you a sizeable sum of money. You know exactly how you want to spend it, and it's not by investing it in the stock market. Your heart is set on a down payment for a house, a new car, a much-needed vacation, or a stylish and expensive new wardrobe.

Response: "No, thank you."

Alert: This is your windfall to invest or squander as you wish, not as your parent wishes. If there's some left over, you can consult with your parent on how to invest it, assuming that's what *you* decide.

● The Scenario

"The house on Glen Ridge Road is so much better than the one you like on Elm Street. We think Glen Ridge is just right for the two of you."

What's going on here: You've been house hunting for almost a year, and you and your husband are in love with the Elm Street house, but your parents think otherwise. For assorted reasons, the house on Elm is exactly what you both want. Your parents, coming from a very different place, envision your family in the Glen Ridge house and point out the flaws in the house you covet. Don't weaken; you are the one who will be living in the house you buy.

Response: "We appreciate your input and pointing out the faults, but no, we really feel strongly the Elm Street house is the one we want."

Alert: Parents who harp can make you wonder if you are making the right choice. Don't be swayed.

The Scenario

"Of course you'll have dessert. It's your favorite; I made it just for you."

What's going on here: You've been dieting and exercising like a pro wrestler to keep your weight in check, but it's hard to refuse the treat itself or your aunt's or mother's or uncle's effort.

Response: "No, thank you. I'm too full." Acknowledge that the dessert is your favorite, thank the cook for her thoughtfulness, and ask to take a slice home (which you can toss on the way).

Alert: Most people are more concerned with appreciation for their culinary accomplishments than they are with your diet struggles. Look out for yourself.

● *The Scenario*

"I need you to help your father."

What's going on here: Your parent thinks you are still twelve years old and she can tell you what to do and you'll do it.

Response: "I'd love to help Dad out, but I can't do what you're asking."

Alert: Be careful not to revert back to your dutiful son or submissive daughter role. Be helpful when you can, but be sure the circumstances fit your schedule and willingness or you will be irritated by most things a parent asks of you.

● *The Scenario*

"Did you make an appointment for your checkup? Do you want me to call the doctor for you?"

What's going on here: Have you lost track of how many times your parent has asked this question? Is he or she still monitoring your health? Hasn't your parent realized you can manage your own medical care issues? Be as determined to make the call yourself as your parent is to make it for you.

Response: "No, thank you. I'll do it."

Alert: Taking charge tells a parent that you are a capable adult no longer in need of a smothering mother hen.

The Scenario

"If it's a boy, Max is nice. And Madeline would be a beautiful name for a baby girl—after Aunt Maddie?"

What's going on here: Your parent is trying to engage you in a baby naming session to find out what names you're considering *and* to be sure you know what names she prefers. Most grandparents would like to have some say in naming your child.

Response: "No. Probably not."

Alert: If you want to keep baby naming between you and your partner, inform your parents and in-laws that you want no help and will tell them the baby's name when he or she is born.

The Scenario

"You're coming home for Easter, I hope."

What's going on here: Your allegiance is being tested. Families and holidays are a sure formula for dicey situations and bruised feelings—and, more often than not, require alterations in traditions. No matter how fair you think you are being and how thoughtful you are in planning holidays, someone will be disappointed or offended.

Response: "No. We're going to my in-laws this year. I know I'm changing what we've always done, but it's unfair for us to celebrate with you every year. We'll be back next Easter."

Alert: People, particularly parents, have difficulty accepting change. You can't make everyone in the family happy all of the time. Stop trying.

Enter the In-Laws

Dealing with in-laws and keeping your own parents satisfied at the same time require a strong will and the ability to firmly call the shots or to be a top-notch negotiator.

In-laws may have different ways of doing things, different points of view, and different expectations of family and family duties. Until you came on the scene, they pretty much ran the family their way; they had a lot more attention from their son or daughter; and while they may adore you (or say they do), you pose a barrier. A son- or daughter-in-law represents changes they may not appreciate or like. Given these realities, in-laws can unsettle your grown-up life, or make your life quite difficult—when you allow it. At those times *no* becomes a very useful tool.

The Scenario

"Brunch as usual?"

What's going on here: When the children were younger, Sunday brunch with your in-laws was fun; it allowed them to see their grandchildren without having to travel. But now the children have activities, practices, and homework, and your in-laws feel insulted when any one of you is missing from the table. You're tired of explaining that your kids are busy or you need to leave right now to pick up your older son from a sleepover at a friend's house. Bottom line: you've come to despise the Sunday brunch ritual.

Response: "Brunch is wonderful, we all enjoyed it, but every Sunday doesn't work for us now that the children are older." (The message should be delivered directly to in-laws via a son or daughter, not by way of the son- or daughter-in-law.)

Alert: When something becomes exasperating rather than pleasurable, it's time to stop.

The Scenario

"We're buying the children the whole train set. Your parents can get them something else," your in-laws tell you.

What's going on here: You know your parents planned on the trains as their gift. There's a competition going on between the in-laws and your parents, and your children are at the center of it. One pair of grandparents is trying to outshine the other in an effort to win over the children. Take charge of the situation before it spins out of control.

Response: "No, my parents want to get them the train set, too. It will be from all the grandparents."

Alert: If parents and in-laws attempt to outdo each other, jump in and act as a referee, being very sure the "players" follow the guidelines you stipulate.

The Scenario

"Don't you think Michele should spend more time job hunting?" your father-in-law asks.

What's going on here: Michele is your sister-in-law, and you don't want to get in the middle of father-daughter, mother-daughter conflicts. Agree, and you're looking for trouble.

Response: "I don't have an opinion."

Alert: You take the chance that your in-law will repeat what you say to your sister-in-law, who will be furious with you for taking sides. In families, who's aligned with whom can change in a flash. Be careful.

The Scenario

"My parents are staying two weeks this year. That's not a problem for you, is it?"

What's going on here: One week seems more than reasonable to put up with any guest. Two weeks of in-laws, no matter how much you love them, can be emotionally taxing, in addition to preparing extra meals and being extra cordial when you get home from work. Here's the clincher: you get along better with your partner's parents than your partner does—they will be picking at each other within two days. So add umpire to your assignment list.

Response: "Have you lost your mind? No, they can't stay that long—and, yes, it's a huge problem."

Alert: It's your home, too, giving you the right to help decide who visits and negotiate how long they stay.

The Scenario

"My mother's expecting us for Christmas week. Will you buy the airline tickets?"

What's going on here: You've spent every Christmas with his family—with pleasure. But you're tired of fighting the Christmas travel crowds with cranky kids. It would be relaxing to be home in your own living room on Christmas morning and to celebrate with your own friends during the holiday week.

Response: "Let's stay home this year. Invite your parents to come here."

Alert: Don't be wishy-washy about decisions that involve changes to expected rituals. Feel free to construct new ones.

No, Darling

In the range of difficulty, refusing the person you live with ranks as high on the scale as refusing a parent. There's that sense of wanting to be there for the person you love and not wanting to disappoint. You float between wanting to make him or her happy and feeling perturbed at not being happy yourself—usually because you are in perpetual motion.

Saying no to a spouse or partner is going to be a bit of a struggle because when you're in love you tend to give in easily. On the flip side, when you agree repeatedly you essentially put yourself last. Isn't it time to step to the front of the line?

When life as a twosome is more equitable, you'll feel less put upon.

The Scenario

"Honey, will you iron my golf slacks?"

What's going on here: You are a devoted wife and mother who allows her husband to golf whenever he wants—which is much more often than you would like. He's on the golf course most of the weekend, leaving you with too many child and household responsibilities. Having to iron his golf attire feels like pouring salt on a wound. Better to teach him how to iron.

Response: "I won't iron your golf pants."

Alert: No matter how much you love your spouse, you don't want to be his subservient butler or his mother!

⬤ The Scenario

"Will you feed Bandit?"

What's going on here: Isn't it enough that you feed the entire family every night? You made it clear when you got the dog that you would only feed two-legged creatures, that the rest of the family would feed the "family dog."

Response: "No, we had a deal."

Alert: It's the simple requests, the ones that you can accomplish in a few minutes, that are thorny. Agree one night and feeding the dog may be on your permanent to-do list along with things like cleaning out the fish tank and taking out the garbage.

⬤ The Scenario

"We're almost finished—only four more boxes. Can't you take a break after we unpack them?"

What's going on here: You've been unpacking for two days and your back hurts, your feet are swollen, your hands are sore, and you're hungry. If you don't sit down and have a snack and rest for ten minutes, you think you will burst into tears.

Response: "I'm taking a break now."

Alert: Statements that say, "This is what I'm doing" make it clear you're not looking for permission. By not asking for permission (or approval) you can't be talked or argued out of what you want to do.

◯ The Scenario

Your ex-husband asks you to call his mother to discuss a problem she has. "You know more about this than anyone else," he says. "Will you advise her?"

What's going on here: Remaining on speaking terms with an ex is admirable. You like his mother and you got along famously, but you've moved on with your life. You miss your mother-in-law, but speaking with her only reminds you of the sorrowful breakup and the sadness you feel.

Response: "I can't. Talking to your mom brings back too many memories. I hope you understand."

Alert: When reminders are painful, it's time to cut off the connection to an ex, including conversations with his or her parents.

◯ The Scenario

"Will you pick up something for dinner?"

What's going on here: It's a given: you are the one who drives fifteen minutes out of your way to pick up take-out when the person you live with drives right by the store.

Response: "No, you'll have to buy dinner tonight. Anything you like is fine with me" or "you know what I like" or "get the usual."

Alert: Don't underestimate your partner's ability to handle chores you routinely do, and don't believe for a second that he's not capable. If you're worried about his choices, give him a list, and praise his selections whatever he unpacks.

The Scenario

"I want to watch the last play of the game. Will you put the chops on the grill?"

What's going on here: Every weekend, all weekend he watches sports. Sporting events and games air round-the-clock. How can every game be so important that you find yourself preparing meals without help? Hint: You are allowing it. Give yourself time to get your emotions in check before you answer.

Response: "Tell me what time you'll be ready. I'll wait."

Alert: Once you make your point, he'll get the picture. (Have a snack if you're hungry.)

The Scenario

"Will you shop for holiday gifts for my boss and assistant?"

What's going on here: You don't know them, and he's stumped for ideas or doesn't want to be bothered thinking about it. You're on your own, and that makes shopping harder, especially for the people on his list that you've never met. It's an impossible task at which you will spend hours meandering through stores. These are his coworkers, not yours.

Response: "No. Not unless you tell me exactly what you want to buy each person" or "not unless you come with me."

Alert: Not everyone views shopping in the same way. Spell it out from your perspective and ask for the direction you need—or flat-out refuse.

⬤ The Scenario

"Nancy, please put those papers away and wipe the kitchen counters before our company arrives."

What's going on here: Your husband has a fetish about messy counters and doesn't want company to see the kitchen in a state of disarray. Why do you always have to clear the counters? It's his mess, too. It's time to change.

Response: "No, honey, you can do that as well as I can. I have to get dressed."

Alert: Old dogs can perform new tricks.

⬤ The Scenario

"There's an office party for the holidays for managers, spouses, and significant others. Will you come with me?"

What's going on here: All your insecurities may come rushing to the surface: What will I say to these people my partner works with? What will I wear? You could feel inadequate and would rather stay home. The stress of pulling yourself together and attending a function you find intimidating is too terrifying.

Response: "No, I really don't want to go."

Alert: It's unlikely that your absence will compromise your husband, wife, or partner's job.

The Scenario

"Will you organize the playroom while I'm gone this weekend?"

What's going on here: You know you can do it faster and better than anyone in your household, but organizing the playroom that only your spouse and children use should be a family project. Fight the urge to clean up even if the mess drives you crazy. Stay out of the playroom.

Response: "No, not without everyone's help. We can all do it when you return from your business trip."

Alert: You're brainwashed. It is not easier to do it yourself and, beyond that, being compulsive is exhausting. Asking for help is a sign of maturity.

With Children—Park Your Guilt

With children, life becomes much harder if you put them and everything else ahead of yourself. When you say yes to your children, they can begin to feel like drill sergeants who control the pace, tenor, and direction of your life: buy me, drive me, help me, finish this for me. By making optimum use of *no* in your interactions with them, you stop being at their mercy and gain deserved time for yourself. Saying no is, plain and simple, your ticket to welcome relief.

At times it feels as if a child's needs or wants involve you in different and demanding ways every waking minute. You have every right to say no to the young child who asks to stay up a few more minutes, as you do to your adult child who seeks a loan from you to start a new venture.

Parenting is a forever proposition. If you want to safeguard your time, save energy, and preserve your resources, make optimum use of *no*. You'll be saying no—or should be—for decades, so park your guilt.

◉ *The Scenario*

"Can I take violin lessons?"

What's going on here: In today's society children, like adults, are overprogrammed. Violin lessons on top of swimming and choir commitments may not be too much for your offspring, but it's too much driving and picking up for you. Two extracurricular activities per child per season are plenty. Think of your schedule first.

Response: "No. We'll talk about it after swim season."

Alert: When you became a parent, you didn't sign on as a full-time chauffeur.

The Scenario

"Mom, I just joined the ski team. We have to buy me new skis before Friday. The coach is giving us racing helmets."

What's going on here: Your child has perfectly fine skis, but claims they're not good enough for racing and his boots aren't good for racing and his poles are too short. The cash register in your brain is on fast-forward as the requests mount. This child has a history of being enthusiastic only to have that zest wane in a month or so.

Response: "Start with the equipment you have (or we'll rent what you need), and then we'll see about buying new."

Alert: Before you invest heavily in a child's new sport or hobby, make sure she's going to stick with it. Set up a trial period of several months, and when you're positive of her commitment, go on a shopping trip.

The Scenario

"The coach wants one of you to be his assistant. Please, will you do it?"

What's going on here: You hate to disappoint your child, but the reality is you can barely make it to the games on a regular basis because you are driving your other child to her extracurricular activities (and possibly bundling the baby into the car, too). Being required to be on the field for every practice and game means finding someone else to drive your younger daughter and/or to babysit.

Response: "Honey, I would love to do that, but it's just not possible."

Alert: Children handle disappointment far better (and faster) than their parents.

The Scenario

"You have to wash my soccer uniform now."

What's going on here: Your child either forgot to tell you he had a game or forgot to get his mud-splattered shorts and shin guards into the hamper.

Response: "No, but I'll show you how to run the washer and dryer."

Alert: Teaching your child laundry basics at an early age will make you feel less like the laundress—and your child feel more independent.

The Scenario

"Mom, can I stay out an hour later tonight? Jamie, Allie, and Erin's parents said yes."

What's going on here: You are responsible for the safety of this teenager who is pressuring you to change her curfew and alter what you believe is a good parenting practice. It's tempting to give in, but don't budge. Soften your *no* with concern.

Response: "No. I'll worry about you too much if you are out so late."

Alert: Guaranteed, your child will keep hounding, but she will find something much more significant than your enforcing a curfew to fault you for later in her life.

◯ The Scenario

"You have to drive me to Andrew's house. It's very necessary," your adolescent implores. His asking fluctuates between whining and hysteria when you won't change your mind.

What's going on here: Few can make a situation appear more critical than the teen who wants to be with his friends to discuss the history assignment or the latest gossip. The begging makes either sound like a catastrophe.

Response: "I can't take you anywhere this afternoon. Between instant messaging and your cell phone, you can be connected and cope with this 'emergency.'"

Alert: Most parents don't like to see their children unhappy for a single second, and for that reason are on twenty-four-hour call to meet their demands. Within half an hour your teen will be content to use the tools he or she has at hand to stay glued to friends and work out the drama of the moment.

The Scenario

"Jerry's picking me up and we're driving over to Nick's house. I'll be home by eight thirty because his parents don't want him driving in the dark yet."

What's going on here: Home before dark doesn't make you less anxious. You're not enthralled with your son accompanying Jerry, who got his license earlier in the week.

Response: "I'll take you to Nick's. Jerry needs more experience behind the wheel before you ride with him."

Alert: Take advantage of the "new driver" leverage you have while you have it. At some point your children's friends won't be novices and you'll be searching for convincing excuses.

The Scenario

"Can I borrow the car tonight?"

What's going on here: Your child wants the car for no particular reason. When you ask why, she answers in vague terms. She and her friends have no plans; they're just "going out," she says.

Response: "The car is transportation to get to and from places. When you decide what you're doing, we can talk about it again."

Alert: Nothing good can come from young people cruising at night. When you know her destination and before she's given the car, insist she call when she arrives and be home at a specific time. Be ironclad about rules relating to the privilege of using the car.

The Scenario

"I have to have it," your ten-year-old announces. *"You could buy it for my birthday."*

What's going on here: The latest game, technological gadget, or fashion "must" is undoubtedly the same one all his friends have or want.

Response: "I don't think so."

Alert: If you give your child every single gizmo he requests, what will he have to look forward to, how will he learn to contribute, to work for what he wants? An outrageous request that is the current craze is a good place to draw the line.

The Scenario

"My friend Tess is driving to the mall this afternoon. Okay if I go with her?"

What's going on here: Permission is sought, and that's commendable. However, you could have things you want your daughter to do, or the roads may be icy, or you think she's shopped enough this month, or you need her to watch her younger brother.

Response: "No."

Alert: If your child pleads, it's your prerogative to be adamant, even testy, by adding, "What part of *no* don't you understand?"

The Scenario

"I don't have too much homework. I'll do it when I get back from the skate park."

What's going on here: His concept of a little homework and yours and his teacher's may be—and usually are—worlds apart.

Response: "No."

Alert: A strong *no* said while looking your child or teen right in the eye sets limits and underscores that you mean what you say. Parents' nos are sound lessons in how the world works—you don't always get what you want.

The Scenario

"Can I rake the leaves later, Dad?" Substitute most anything you ask your children to do: clean their rooms, set the table, do the dishes, sweep the porch, mow the lawn, pull the weeds, water the garden, take out the garbage. The operative word here *is* later.

What's going on here: Asking for a postponement is a stall. Your child hopes you forget about the chore, or better yet get aggravated and do it yourself. He's banking on one or the other happening, and in a busy parent's life your child comes out the winner if you agree to any form of procrastination.

Response: "No."

Alert: Children are specialists in avoiding tasks that smack of work. Have them do it when asked, no negotiation.

The Scenario

"It's not fair: I want to go to bed when Katie does. It doesn't matter if she's older than me!"

What's going on here: Sibling rivalry takes many forms. From a child's point of view you are giving an older child preferential treatment with a later bedtime. She'll fight you on this one.

Response: "No. You need the extra sleep to help you grow. When you are Katie's age, you can stay up later."

Alert: For the present you are the parent who would like an hour or so to yourself in the evening. Don't be ashamed of being and acting like the boss of your young children.

The Scenario

"Can I spend the night at Tom's?"

What's going on here: Your son wants to spend the night at a friend's house, but you have only met Tom once and his parents never. That's sufficient to prompt your answer.

Response: "No, your friend can sleep over here if you like."

Alert: Follow your internal warnings, and don't think about your decision too long. It's probably a good one.

The Scenario

"Billy asked me out for Friday night. Can I go?" your twelve-year-old asks.

What's going on here: You wrestle with the shock of thinking your daughter may be old enough to date. Conflict emerges: she's definitely too young. On the other hand, you have to let her grow up, but a preteen is too young to date, you conclude. Your little girl is not dating, not yet.

Response: "My answer is no. You'll have to give me details about this date before I'll reconsider."

Alert: Before you fly off the handle at the very concept of your daughter going out with a boy, find out what "dating" means to your child and her friends. Could be that a group of friends is gathering at someone's home or are going to the movies en masse. Group dating is not necessarily dating as you knew it.

The Scenario

"Can I wear makeup? I'm a teenager now."

What's going on here: Your just-turned teenager thinks lipstick and blush with a tad of mascara will enhance her looks. You're appalled at her being a painted lady at age thirteen. Yet, you've noticed her friends have begun to wear makeup.

Response: "That's not an idea I'm overjoyed by. My overall reaction is no, but let's talk about it."

Alert: You're bucking peer pressure, and your teen will think you are being unreasonable if you flat-out refuse. View her asking as an opportunity to influence her makeup choices and to teach her the proper way as you see it to apply cosmetics. Consider giving her the go-ahead with the limitations you feel are appropriate—not to school, not to family functions, not on whatever occasions that will make you uncomfortable.

◯ *The Scenario*

Your children beg, "Can we get a dog?" They pledge to take care of him.

What's going on here: In theory, the children mean what they say. They think they will attend to the new pet, but as parents, you'll be doing 95 percent of the caretaking no matter what they promise. Don't agree unless *you* would like a dog.

Response: "No." Then, add all your practical reasons for the decision: we work, the dog would be home alone too much, everyone's schedules are full, we don't have sufficient yard space, and you have allergies.

Alert: While the dog may not need frequent walks in his youth, when older and your children are off to college, the dog could want out six or seven times a day.

⬤ The Scenario

"Mom, I have to start my homework. I have tons. Will you do my dishes?"

What's going on here: When the question comes accompanied by his charming smile and maybe a peck on the cheek as he bolts from the table and for the door, you could so easily agree.

Response: "No way. Get back here, clear your dishes, and put them in the dishwasher."

Alert: If you allow small leniencies, you're putting yourself on the fast track to indentured servitude.

⬤ The Scenario

"It's out of state, but I want to go to college with Don and Wesley," announces your soon-to-be high school graduate.

What's going on here: Your son has been visiting colleges with friends. Like many young people who aren't sure what they want to study, he and his buddies are attracted to the colleges reputed to be the best party schools, but you refuse to pay out-of-state tuition unless you're convinced he'll be serious about getting an education.

Response: "No, we're not spending money for you to go on vacation for four years."

Alert: You don't have to defend your position. Be firm. Your decision is not open to debate when you're bankrolling the college bills.

The Scenario

"Mom and Dad, will you give me money for the down payment on a house?"

What's going on here: You are not shocked by this request from your adult child. After all you've been financing her expensive lifestyle for decades, if not wholly, then certainly in part.

Response: "No, we aren't paying your down payment."

Alert: Be sure you are really helping when you come to a child's financial aid, whatever his or her age. Be certain requested money won't deplete the dollars you've put aside for retirement, and if it won't, think about whether or not it's time this adult child took care of her own monetary needs.

3

At Work

You will want to apply many of the insights and techniques for saying no to friends and family in your business life as well. Doing so aids in making the best use of your time, being firm about the direction you want to go, and staying focused on achieving the goals you set for yourself.

These business-related examples will help you identify what falls within the purview of your job and reject tasks that don't without harming your position or credibility with your boss or coworkers. You'll be better equipped to accept and tend to assignments that gain their respect and move you forward. You'll also learn that you don't have to be aggressive, defensive, or offensive when you refuse.

Your tone of voice and body language are far more influential in sending your *no* message than the actual words—*how* you say no makes it more acceptable.

Whether you are the CEO, an aspiring CEO, or the most recent person hired, you want to be a team player, want your group to be productive and your company to thrive. The consensus thinking in business is that agreeing to demands and requests no matter how absurd keeps bosses and clients happy. Such thinking is antiquated and can reap disastrous results. Here's why:

By assuming too much responsibility and being perpetually gracious about taking on more work, to whom do you think bosses and coworkers will turn when something has to get done? And to whom will they point when something goes amiss? You, of course. Maybe you are a performance junkie who fears people will dislike you or consider you an underachiever, or you worry your job will be in jeopardy if you say no. At this point, you may have gone so far that you define yourself by your accomplishments rather than by who you really are. In most jobs people are defined by what they produce, but:

If you stretch yourself too thin, you run the risk of making mistakes or doing a mediocre job.

Everyone in the office perceives you as the picture of efficiency. You dive in and take over when no one else comes forward. You do so without being asked. The staff counts on you. You're not the office manager, but you make sure that the place runs like well-oiled machinery, despite the miniscule budget. There is no such thing as being too responsible. However, you need to be assertive and able to say no in the event that your company, no matter what its size, and the people you work with ask for everything you are willing to give and then some.

Before you say yes, think strategically about what you agree to and what advantage it holds for you.

Being cautious and realistic about taking on too much simplifies the process of saying no and prevents you from doing a shoddy job that may be detrimental to your career in the long run.

High Performance Versus Overload

The boss and her boss sing your praises. What a good feeling. Or is it? What is it costing you? You perform at peak levels, but the added stress creates myriad negative reactions that affect your sleep, your diet, or your anxiety level—all of which can lead to errors in judgment on the job.

Such high performance levels play havoc with your personal life, too—you're frequently late, forced to cancel dates, or spend too little time with family and friends, who feel slighted. But most important, if you overextend yourself and become ill, you are of no help to anyone. Instead of mucking about in a quandary over whether or not to say no, just spit it out and avoid unnecessary obligations that hold no possible benefit for you. If the boss is asking, negotiate a solution that takes you out of the picture but still gets the task accomplished.

Often bosses and colleagues in higher positions know when they are asking something beyond the normal range of what is expected. Listen for apology in their voices, a slight reluctance to ask, a telltale wavering. Each is a clue that your *no* will be accepted without challenge or consequence. In the very least, you'll know your superior is open to alternatives.

The Scenario

"The reception area is a mess. Would you clean it up before the clients arrive?" the office manager asks with noticeable hesitation.

What's going on here: It's a small staff and everyone has to pitch in; you don't mind being the maid now and then, but not for every client meeting and not when the others regularly do their vanishing act. You've been pegged because of your willingness to complete the little things in the office that those you work with choose to ignore or avoid. The office manager knows this is not the best use of your time.

Response: "No, I'm rushing to a meeting. Can you ask someone else?" "I have to make a phone call." "I'm on my way to check that all the documentation is in order. Can you ask someone else?"

Alert: Don't make a practice of covering up for the shirkers, or you'll be doing double duty for a very long time.

● *The Scenario*

"Do me a favor and go over Tim's report and let me know what you think. It's an imposition, I know, but . . ."

What's going on here: (Note: the asker's wavering.) Tim doesn't work in your department, and you're not entirely sure what his report is about. The person asking may be trying to protect himself by getting another opinion. You also don't want to encroach in someone else's territory. Provide a rationale when you can.

Response: "No, I don't know enough about this project to give a sound review. Someone in Tim's department could provide a more objective review."

Alert: Masquerading as a know-it-all backfires eventually. Saying, "I don't know enough" is acceptable. You gain more points for honesty.

The Scenario

The boss requests the year-end analysis. "Can you have it to me by Friday?"

What's going on here: You've known the due date for months, but haven't worked on it because he's given you other more pressing assignments. The boss knows you're not a slacker; if you could work up what he needs by Friday, you would. Promise the year-end analysis for Friday and be up all night for the next few nights. It's more wise to be straightforward and see what the boss wants you to do.

Response: "No, I won't have it ready. I need an extension."

Alert: Making promises you can't fulfill makes you look incompetent. Keep your boss informed when new projects interfere with or will slow down others. Negotiate a new due date.

The Scenario

The person you work for says, "A new client, a rush job. Can you take it on?"

What's going on here: You can feel the weight of the job as soon as the question hits your ears. You can't imagine squeezing in one more client, and a rush job to boot. Before answering think about what's on your plate already and if this new client may or may not move you in the direction of your goals.

Response: "Not me. Not unless you take me off several other projects."

Alert: When you carry a full load, doing more doesn't necessarily equate to increased job security. It will, however, greatly add to your anxiety and exhaustion.

The Scenario

"This mailing is huge and has to go out by the end of the day. Will you stuff envelopes during lunch?"

What's going on here: A reputation for reliability is usually a plus, but not when peers turn to you regularly for the tedious jobs. To break the cycle, start refusing chores that earn you nothing more than a pat on the back. Keep your *no* simple.

Response: "No, I can't do that today."

Alert: As soon as coworkers pick up on the fact that you're no longer willing to take on the grunt work as a matter of course, they'll hesitate before asking. The sooner and more often you make them aware, the faster they will get the message. Bosses are a different story; tread lightly with the nos when they ask for the small stuff.

The Scenario

"The printer's out of ink!"

What's going on here: A colleague is perched on the threshold to your office. The panic in her voice is telling— she has to print a job right away. If it's not the printer needing a cartridge, it's someone wanting help with a spreadsheet or presentation software. You've been pegged the office techie, and the staff, from the president on down, seeks you out. But where is the polite, "I'm in a bind. Can you please help me? I know you're busy, but this is an emergency."

Response: "I can't do it this minute, but as soon as I'm free I'll show you how so you can do it yourself in the future." You can also say in your best matter-of-fact voice, "It's quite simple. Open the machine and follow the printed instructions on the lid or side. Let me know if you still have a problem."

Alert: Don't assume that what a colleague is doing is more urgent than your work. You belittle your importance by rescuing everyone who asks and will wind up taking work home most nights.

The Scenario

"A new assistant starts in the morning. I'd like you to train her."

What's going on here: The whole staff knew you back when you were the brand-new assistant and still sees you in that job sometimes. You've worked your way up, taken on more responsibility and gotten several promotions to the impressive position you hold now. You are a long way from that desk outside a manager's office, but you know the procedures and are an excellent teacher.

Response: "I'd be happy to, but I have a presentation tomorrow (an appointment, a big job to finish). I really can't take the time away from my projects. Don't you think she'd feel more comfortable learning from another assistant?"

Alert: Once you're pegged as the trainer, you will have to remind people subtly that that's not your job anymore.

The Scenario

"Can you help me finish up the Johnson project?"

What's going on here: You really can't. As much as you would like to help your colleague, the way the week is panning out, you'll be lucky to polish off what's urgent on your own desk. Letting a person know that what you want is important to you carries a lot of weight and makes refusing more acceptable. Before you refuse, be sure that your *no* won't negatively affect your group or team.

Response: "I want to help you, but it's important to me to finish what I have to do."

Alert: Saying no is a time management issue; pay attention to your commitments before accepting more. Setting new limits may be in order to get you out from under the yeses that define and bury you at—and in—work.

The Scenario

"Lawrence resigned, and I'm going to redistribute his workload between you and Allison."

What's going on here: You knew Lawrence planned to leave, but you didn't think his work would be passed to you. You can't refuse, but you need to get additional information.

Response: "How long before we hire Lawrence's replacement?" Or, "Is this a temporary assignment?" Or, "You'll have to tell me what you want done first since doing his work will put some of mine behind schedule."

Alert: Questions about how long you are expected to cover for an employee who leaves lets your boss know that additional work will be a struggle. Asking for a priority agenda will lower his deadline expectations and give you a bit of breathing room.

◯ *The Scenario*

"Will you speak at the Colorado conference in November?"

What's going on here: Although you dislike giving presentations, in your mind, November, six months away, will seemingly never come. Who plans or worries so far in advance? While you're agreeing, you look like a gem of a person, a hero for filling in a vacant slot on the conference schedule.

Response: "Thank you for the opportunity, I really appreciate it, but I have to pass."

Alert: When a chore is to take place in the future, the tendency is to think about it in a generalized way, rather than about the hassles and problems involved in its execution. As the conference draws closer and the amount of work you will need to do becomes paramount, you may begin to feel anxious and upset with yourself for committing—a feeling hardly worth the good impression you made or praise you received months earlier.

◯ *The Scenario*

"I'm offering you more territory (an extra class to teach, a high-level class, a better schedule). What do you think?"

What's going on here: Sometimes offers are phrased to sound like bonuses or promotions. It's inviting to jump at the chance to do something different. Unless you're familiar with the job, you're apt to be taken by surprise—and taken in. You'd best find out before committing.

Response: "What a nice proposition. I can't say yes or no just yet. I'll get back to you in a couple days."

Alert: Be sure what's being offered is really an improvement or step up in some way. Are there financial gain possibilities or career enhancement in the offer immediately or down the road?

◯ *The Scenario*

"I really need this job. Can you hire me on a trial basis?"

What's going on here: You desperately need help and she has a great résumé and seems a decent person. However, you sense a bit of aggressiveness that might work in another department, but not in the department with the opening. The applicant's forwardness is going to grate on the other people she'll be working with. Your current employees will be happier if you keep them in mind when you answer.

Response: "You're just not right for our needs at the moment."

Alert: Always go with your gut reaction, particularly when you know the other personalities involved, even if it means everyone will have to work a bit harder until you find the right person.

The Scenario

"I'm thinking about starting a sign-in and sign-out system for middle managers and support staff. You'll have to tell your group."

What's going on here: The person you work for has decided that productivity will increase if employees are forced to be in at nine and finish up at five. You know the people in your department will resent "punching a clock" and it will reduce their output and loyalty to you. With one or two exceptions, they give you far more than an eight-hour day. You have to protect them by avoiding time sheets.

Response: "The people who work for me don't need to be monitored. They're professionals; they don't need a mother."

Alert: Stand up for your employees and let the boss be the heavy who makes the announcement if you can't prevent a timed workday. If it's a couple of people's tardiness that is prompting the change, offer to deal with them separately. But don't penalize the entire group.

The Scenario

"Let's meet first thing in the morning. Nine o'clock is good for me."

What's going on here: Assuming this associate is not your immediate superior, you can say first thing isn't good for you—you might have to work late to prepare for the meeting or to catch up on outstanding work.

Response: "If you don't mind, let's meet at nine-thirty." If you feel you *must* offer an explanation, go with something along the lines of, "The extra half hour will let me review what we need to address, and the meeting will go faster."

Alert: There's a good chance your coworker will be amenable to half an hour leeway.

The Scenario

"Is this a good time to talk?"

What's going on here: When you're distracted, when you're trying to get something off your desk, the tendency is to fall right into the conversation rather than risk offending the person on the other end of the line. You think it will only take a minute; you'll get rid of the caller quickly (that rarely happens). You will be much more focused on the caller and the content of the call if you arrange another time to talk.

Response: "I have to call you back."

Alert: If the caller, even a superior, has the decency to ask if you are available, she won't be offended if you put her off for twenty minutes or an hour.

● *The Scenario*

"Please call this client back for me. He's really difficult. Since he doesn't know you as well, maybe he'll just take the information and not ask his usual hundred questions."

What's going on here: You have your own impossible clients, but you don't look around the office for a stool pigeon to make calls for you, and neither should your coworker. Without telling him so, give him options that don't involve you.

Response: "Why don't you send him an e-mail? Or, send a fax? It will seem awfully odd if I call."

Alert: Offering plausible alternatives voices your refusal and keeps you out of no-win situations without having to say, "Are you kidding? What makes you think I'm going to do the unpleasant part of your job for you?"

The Scenario

"I have another question. Do you have a minute?"

What's going on here: It's not yet noon and the guy in the next cubicle has been in yours four times with different questions on the same problem. At this point you want to say, "Just leave it on my desk and I'll do it." Don't.

Response: "Work with the information you have and we'll talk later."

Alert: You have to take a strong stand in order to get your own work done and not be manipulated into doing someone else's work.

The Scenario

"Will you help me put together a speech for my meeting? It won't take long."

What's going on here: You know better. Before you can begin to be of any help, you will need to understand the background of the business, charity, or event, the focus of his speech, and some things about his audience.

Response: "I don't know anything about your project and don't have the time to learn it now."

Alert: Don't agree to do things for which the learning curve is too steep or too time-consuming unless you see a strong and beneficial reason to do so.

The Scenario

"How about we work on this project together?"

What's going on here: When confronted by a coworker you know is irresponsible, doesn't carry his own weight in joint efforts, or whose work ethic drives you crazy, protect yourself when you answer.

Response: "No, I told Amy I'd work with her." Or, "I'm probably going to work with Tyrone." Or, "I can't take on anything else right now."

Alert: You don't ever have to provide lengthy excuses, and you certainly don't want to say anything hurtful to the other person when you decline.

The Scenario

"If I help you, we will create a more thorough and professional-looking presentation."

What's going on here: People have different work styles— yours is fast and efficient; his is slow and plodding. Neither of you is likely to change. If you're thinking, I might as well do this assignment myself for all he's going to add, refuse.

Response: "Thanks for offering, but I can handle it."

Alert: Avoid working with someone who will not only frustrate you but also slow you down, no matter how much you like him or her personally.

Mixing Business with Pleasure

What seems a pleasant invitation to some could feel like a major intrusion to you. Social situations that correspond with business are open to interpretation. If you're friendly with a coworker, attending her wedding will be delightful; if the coworker is just another person in the office to you, the wedding will be an annoyance and take away weekend time when you have much more important or fun things on tap. If you are clear about the people at work you consider personal friends versus those you view primarily as business associates, deciding whether or not to mix your business and social life is less complicated. Unless the decision will affect your job standing in some way, you will be more inclined to spend out-of-office time with those who have the dual standing of coworker and friend.

No matter what the status of the people involved, make sure you know what's going on before you object to what you are being asked. Even when you are adamant about keeping your social life separate, that questionable command performance crops up. But if you're like most people, there's a fine line between those at work in your friend category and those you would rather not spend off-duty hours with if you don't have to.

Saying no is easier if you consider ahead of time how you feel about mixing your social life and your business life and make unambiguous distinctions between friend and colleague.

Predetermining your business inner circle as well as your position on moral issues revolving around business accomplishes two goals: you know what you want and what you are willing to do and with whom, and you're less likely to be pulled into situations in which you chastise yourself for not having considered the inconvenience or possible repercussions.

⬤ The Scenario

An e-mail arrives inviting you to join several colleagues for lunch. "It will be such fun to see everyone. Are you available November 5th, 7th, or 8th?"

What's going on here: You are on such overload, you think, one more lunch, no big deal. You like these associates, particularly because you don't work with them regularly. But did you stop to think why this gathering is being arranged? Does one of them routinely rope you into volunteering time you don't have or frequently ask for business-related information you're not at liberty to give?

Response: "Thanks for including me, but I can't squeeze another thing into my crammed schedule that week."

Alert: If there's a chance you're going to be bamboozled into something, say no.

⬤ The Scenario

"We should carpool to work. I practically go right past your house."

What's going on here: Sharing the commute does have its advantages—company when you're stuck in traffic, time to rehash the day's events or to discuss work-related problems, and paying half the amount for gas. Yet you know yourself: you'll be nervous if he's a few minutes late to pick you up, if you want to leave early if you have a meeting, or if you stay late to finish up whatever you're involved in. You won't be able to make spur-of-the moment decisions to go out after work or come in a bit later if you've been out on the town the night before. You may prefer to listen to a book on tape or to a news program rather than talk about the office.

Response: "It's a good idea, but my hours are too erratic." Or, "I use the time to unwind and listen to music. Thanks for asking."

Alert: If you think your flexibility will be curtailed or the arrangements and last-minute schedule changes will be a hassle, drive yourself.

The Scenario

"You work out at the gym up the street, don't you? Being your gym buddy would motivate me to exercise and, boy, could I use it."

What's going on here: You relish your forty-five-minute spin class away from the office and don't need any other inducement to get you there. You like going alone; it gives you a chance to think about something besides work. You return to your desk refreshed and ready for whatever the afternoon has in store.

Response: "It's the only time I have to myself all day. It's nothing personal. I hope you understand."

Alert: Be protective of the little private time you have during the day.

The Scenario

Olivia drops two resort brochures on your desk and says, "Come with me. We'll have such a good time."

What's going on here: You're friendly with Olivia, but not *that* friendly. Sharing a room, lazing on a beach, and three meals a day is more bonding time than you want with anyone in your office. Nine to five Monday through Friday and occasional drinks after work are enough togetherness.

Response: "These places look fabulous, but I'm set for vacation this year." Or, "I usually go on holiday with old friends." Or, "I prefer to go away by myself." Or, "I'm using my vacation for family obligations." Or, "Those places are more money than I want to spend." Or, "I'm staying home this year to save for Cancún." (Go with the truth.)

Alert: Being with coworkers out of the office is not part of the job. If the thought of a coworker getting too close worries you, don't entertain the idea of vacationing together. Away from the office you may be inclined to offer more details of your life than you want known.

◯ *The Scenario*

"We're having a baby shower for Ellen the last Saturday of this month. You'll be there, yes?"

What's going on here: Between work-related weddings, birthdays, dinners, Friday night beers, and weekend parties you could virtually wipe personal friends out of your life. If you say yes to one office-related invitation, are you obligated to the others? How do you draw the line without offending someone?

Response: "I can't be there, but I want to chip in on the gift."

Alert: Figure out which people are key to your position and which people you classify as friends to help you decide the festivities you must attend.

◯ *The Scenario*

"See you at the office party?"

What's going on here: Office parties are rarely command appearances; we just think they are. If you're married with children or have other social obligations, bosses and colleagues will understand your absence. And if you don't like parties, don't go. Most companies evaluate performance during business hours, not on how well you socialize or move on the dance floor.

Response: "I won't be able to make it this year."

Alert: Two days after the party few, if anyone, will remember whether or not you were there.

The Scenario

"We're taking you to lunch. We won't take no for an answer."

What's going on here: You're dieting and planned a yogurt to get you through until dinner; you're going out for a big dinner; you don't feel like going out; you're too busy. Your choices for what you do during your free time are removed when coworkers mandate what you will do.

Response: "Thank you, but I'm staying in today."

Alert: Only you are in charge of you, and that gives you options. Exercise them. When pressured tell yourself you will not be worn down.

The Scenario

"Leave your cell phone on this weekend. We may need you."

What's going on here: You're not a physician and you're not a fireman or police officer or any type of service person who must be available for emergencies. In your business, there are few crises in the true sense of the word. Whatever this person could possibly want can wait until Monday.

Response: "I have a busy weekend planned. If I don't pick up, leave a message that I may or may not have time to return."

Alert: Alter a request to make it—or part of it—acceptable and manageable. There has to be a limit to how much of your life you are willing to give to your job. Emergencies or rush projects aside, getting work-related calls on the weekend is an invasion of privacy and beyond the call of duty.

Power Plays

Many of the problems encountered in the work environment come from the people in charge, the people you work for who laud their position and the power it gives them over you. For some of them, work is their life; their very being is synonymous with the office or their job. They've adopted the culture and it infiltrates their social life; their business and personal lives are one and the same. When a person's world revolves around work and being successful, his or her demands can be unreasonable. Requests that come with hidden agendas rarely work in your favor.

In the world of work—and out of it—nervy people ask just about anything of anybody. They continually overstep your boundaries and think nothing of it. Getting others to do something for them or using their power to get what they want is how "users" operate. If they are accustomed to having it their way with you, it's time to change that. Negotiate alternatives by being very clear about the change you want.

You can be just as effective in saying no without using the *no* word.

The Scenario

At four-thirty the boss asks, "Can you stay a few extra hours tonight?"

What's going on here: Tough to refuse the boss, tougher still if you've made other plans. You wonder if a *no* endangers your job security, but not showing up for your evening plans may jeopardize a friendship or your love life. It's unlikely that turning down the boss's last-minute request will put you in front of the firing squad. A qualified *no* is in order.

Response: "I'd like to but can't tonight: I have plans, but any other night this week is fine."

Alert: Weigh the situation to see if you are really needed or if your loyalty is being tested. Run a mental checklist: What work is outstanding? What are the due dates? Can you finish up during the day? Anything major upcoming that requires more than the normal preparation: a conference; a presentation; out-of-town clients visiting? Or, is this your boss's standard request because he doesn't have a life beyond the office? Is it his personality? Some bosses like to flaunt their power and/or see how committed you really are.

◯ *The Scenario*

"I know you don't want to do this, but would you transcribe the tape from yesterday's session?"

What's going on here: The significant words are not what you are being asked to do, but how you are being asked. "I know you don't want to do this" and prefaces like it cleverly break down your resistance to the question. By telling you he understands you don't want to do something, he gets you to lower your guard. You think, he's reluctant to ask, how nice.

Response: "I'm backed up as it is; I don't know when I can get to the tape."

Alert: Listen for statements that chisel away at your resistance and aim to make you more willing.

◯ *The Scenario*

"I only trust you to call these people."

What's going on here: What a joke; who's she kidding? There are other people equally qualified and experienced to make the calls.

Response: "Tim can handle those calls as well as I can."

Alert: Make it clear that you're on to the game of flattery without saying so. Give suggestions on how the task can be accomplished to free yourself.

● *The Scenario*

"Great job, good weekend conference, lots of fun. See you in the office Monday morning."

What's going on here: You have just devoted your weekend to your boss, his demands, and the company's agenda. He views the convention as time off, but you've been talking to clients, smiling, and doing business since Friday morning without so much as a quiet dinner—hardly a relaxing weekend.

Response: "I think we made great progress, but I really need a day to recharge. If it's okay with you, I'm taking Monday off."

Alert: Without a break from business, you run the risk of burnout. Before a retreat or conference, prearrange time off if you have an employer who doesn't think you need it.

● *The Scenario*

A client calls, yelling into the phone, "Things changed on our end; send everything overnight to me so I have it in the morning. No excuses, I mean it, or you're fired."

What's going on here: The difficult client: he's been that way since day one. He drives you and your staff to the limits. At some point you have to ask yourself if the money is worth the aggravation. Wouldn't the office be better off if you expended your energy finding a more pleasant and reasonable client?

Response: "It won't be ready. We were told we had until the end of the week, and we'll be ready then or before."

Alert: Threats and intimidation tactics create incredible strain and stress. Do you need such an inflexible client? Before you dump the client, evaluate the financial loss, decide how to replace him, and make sure that everyone who should be involved in the decision is consulted.

◯ The Scenario

"Can you cover the Toronto meeting for me? I'll owe you one."

What's going on here: As with personal friends, there are those who make across-the-board, vacant promises. Be sure this one's for real by asking . . .

Response: "I'll take you up on the offer. Can you cover the Atlanta meeting for me?"

Alert: Test people's word beforehand, not after. If you can't be assured of quid pro quo, *no* will slide right out of your mouth.

◯ The Scenario

"You have to bring in more contracts (clients, business, jobs). I don't care how you get them."

What's going on here: Without actually saying so, the person you work for is telling you to employ any method possible, aboveboard or not. He's out-and-out bullying you into using tactics you don't agree with, feel are wrong, or know are unethical.

Response: "We need to talk about this; I can't work that way."

Alert: When asked to do something unethical, you must address the suggestion head-on. Making your position clear tells the boss that he can't bully you or ask you to compromise your principles. You've announced the line you will not cross.

The Scenario

"You'll be getting a 2 percent raise starting with your next paycheck."

What's going on here: In every organization, some employees are worth more than others. And almost everyone thinks they are worth more than they are paid. Make sure you know your value to the company before you answer.

Response: "Thank you, but I think my ability is as strong as anyone else's. I've made huge contributions and done good work this year—better than a 2 percent raise indicates."

Alert: Your value to a company is not what *you* think, but what your employer thinks. If you overestimate your importance to the operation, you could be job hunting shortly. Be very cautious.

The Scenario

"When you go to lunch, would you pick up a bottle of aspirin and a pair of black pantyhose for me?"

What's going on here: You are an assistant, *not* a personal assistant. There's no reason you have to buy deodorant, pantyhose, or nail polish for your boss. Nor do you have to do a dry cleaner run or walk the boss's dog.

Response: "I brought my lunch today and am not going out of the building." Or, "I'm meeting someone for lunch and won't have time." Or, "If I do that, I won't be able to finish the work you've given me."

Alert: Start being your boss's personal shopper and errand runner, and the next thing you know you'll spend lunch hours buying kitty litter for her cat and get-well cards for her sick relatives.

The Scenario

"Will you take our new employee under your wing tomorrow and introduce her to everyone?"

What's going on here: Your desk is piled high with incomplete jobs and you definitely weren't assigned to the welcoming committee, nor do you want to be. Your superior has it in his or her head that you represent the company well, including making people feel comfortable—a task usually handled by the human resource department.

Response: "Not tomorrow! I'm swamped."

Alert: Communicate why you are too busy. Smart bosses want productivity and will realize someone less critical to the business can be the welcome wagon.

The Scenario

"I'm coming with you to the meeting. I'll be there to back you up and give support."

What's going on here: Colleagues who are excessively involved in your career can be intrusive to a point that you feel stifled. They stick with you every step of the way because they think they are shielding you, because they feel and act like your parent, or because they believe associating with you makes them look important.

Response: "It's so nice of you to offer, but I have to tackle this one myself."

Alert: Decide if this person is being truly supportive or if he is latching on to your favorable position in the company— to what he construes as your current or future success.

Sticky Situations

Although most problems and requests at work could be classified as sticky situations, the ones presented here pull you in different directions. Some contain an appealing element that's hard to resist; others put you in conflict or in a compromising or uncomfortable position.

Sticky situations can put your job at risk or disrupt your goals. Although they appear to be straightforward, many times they are layered with nuances that are difficult to sort out. For example, an office mate who was also a personal friend but left the company some months ago asks you to send her confidential information to which she had access before she took another job. What do you do?

A *no* allows you to retain your integrity and keep a realistic workload that leaves you less stressed and better able to handle the unexpected.

Be mindful when work and private life responsibilities compete for your time.

The Scenario

"One of my best people just quit. Can you take over for him? It's a better route and will mean top dollar to you."

What's going on here: You've only had this job a short time, so it feels like an offer you can't refuse. You've produced and the boss wants to give you a premier position with more responsibility and more money—and considerably more time on the road, three to five days versus the one or two with your current position. You think anyone in his right mind would say yes. Think again. You know you can handle it but have grave concerns. You're in a new relationship that looks as if it could go places, which it won't if you're on the road all week every week; perhaps you're in a new marriage; maybe you had a baby recently or have young children you want to watch grow up.

Response: "I'm really flattered that you think so highly of me, but I can't handle the additional travel right now. Thank you so much."

Alert: Analyze attractive proposals and the effect on your career *and* on your personal life so you don't wind up feeling overly burdened or putting your personal life in peril.

● *The Scenario*

"I found the perfect job for me at the same place your friend Stella works. I'm applying for it. Will you be one of my references or call Stella and ask her to put in a good word for me?"

What's going on here: You're in a precarious position because you don't classify this person's work as superior. She's not a close friend, and you don't want to go out on a limb for her. If you call Stella, you're putting your reputation on the line. If she doesn't work out, Stella will never trust your recommendations again.

Response: A noncommittal answer is called for. "I don't think Stella's in a position to help very much." Or, "Let me think how I can approach Stella." Or, the self-protective standby, "I'm not going to be very influential. You should be able to get a stronger reference than I'll be."

Alert: Within any given field, the business world is small. You never know when you may be changing jobs, and recommending people you don't have faith in could reflect negatively on your ability to judge people.

The Scenario

"Do you like this design?"

What's going on here: You dislike it intensely and think it's all wrong for its intended purpose, but you are fearful of wounding its creator's ego and/or never being asked for your opinion again.

Response: "I have some reservations" (not an off-putting *no*, but a *no* that gets your point across).

Alert: If you're going to have to work with or live with the design (or a business decision that impacts you) for a long time, you need to express your thoughts and offer constructive criticism.

The Scenario

"I'm adding my name to the finished report, if it's okay with you."

What's going on here: Sure, she helped pull the loose ends together, checked the punctuation, and ran off the copies. She made a useful suggestion in the content, but one out of fifty ideas doesn't merit a full credit line. She's being bold and stretching the importance of her contribution.

Response: Smile warmly and say, "Not on this one. I worked too long and too hard."

Alert: If your hard work is the major mark of the report, don't allow others who don't really deserve it to dilute your effort—or praise if there's any coming.

The Scenario

"I need to leave early. Will you tell the boss I wasn't feeling well if she asks?"

What's going on here: Your colleague never looked healthier. He's asking you to cover for him and to jeopardize your standing with a superior. In plain language, he's asking you to lie for him and probably wouldn't do the same for you. Most important, he won't like you any better or any less if you refuse.

Response: "I don't feel good about doing that. Why don't you leave the boss a note?"

Alert: Don't compromise your principles to bail out someone else.

The Scenario

"Please e-mail me the numbers from the Freeman file I was working on before I started my new job. I'll return the favor."

What's going on here: You work with sensitive and confidential data and information. You know you are not supposed to give out any details, and certainly not the type of material your former colleague wants.

Response: "If I send what you want, I could lose my job. You don't want that."

Alert: Protect your position within the company. A breach of confidence is not worth it, whatever the payback.

The Scenario

"Will you stay tonight so we can wrap up this program?"

What's going on here: The program has been dragging for months, you have devoted more time than you wanted to it and have made significant contributions. It's doubtful a few more hours will make a difference, and if that time is crucial, the others can handle any missing details.

Response: "The program is in good shape; you can finish without me."

Alert: Remind yourself that your imprint is already bold and clear on a particular program.

The Scenario

"Can you give me the recipe for the brownies you brought over last week?"

What's going on here: Midmorning calls interrupt your flow, and callers often talk endlessly, not respecting the fact that you work from home. The prevailing misconception is that you have all the time in the world. You don't want to be abrupt or condescending, but you'll get nothing accomplished if you stop what you're doing to find the recipe or supply the carpool schedule your friend misplaced.

Response: "I can't give it to you now; I'm really busy. I'll call you tonight."

Alert: People have a difficult time understanding the work-from-home concept unless you establish boundaries to claim your office hours as off-limits for personal calls and interruptions. You have to be disciplined and strong in the face of diversions so others respect your pressures and goals.

The Scenario

"We need help with the corporate holiday fund-raiser. Which committee would you like to be on?"

What's going on here: When you're asked to lend a hand, remind yourself and the person asking that you can't fit another task into your overbooked workday or life.

Response: "I'm just too busy. I'm overextended as it is."

Alert: A printed schedule of appointments and commitments taped above your computer or workspace will keep you from falling prey to unrealistic expectations that serve others and not yourself. You can contribute without being on a time-consuming committee.

◯ The Scenario

"You can't leave us," the members of your professional organization (could be an investment or other club) beg you. "Please stay?"

What's going on here: You've been in this group many years, its members feel like family. But, the big but: you've been wrestling with the amount of preparation time stolen out of your workweek and the valuable information and advice you give versus what you get. Bottom line, the two don't equalize no matter how you try to weigh your feeling that you are letting down the other members. After years of being together, you know your contribution is more valuable than what you get in return.

Response: "No, I can't do this anymore. I'll miss you all and our meetings."

Alert: All you have is your time. Once you get those hours back, you won't feel like a deserter for very long.

◯ The Scenario

"My friend's writing a book. Would you look at the manuscript and tell her what she needs to do?"

What's going on here: You're an editor (lawyer, decorator, mechanic, builder, electrician, landscape architect) by profession. You don't ask your friend the doctor to see one of your friends for free. People frequently and innocently ask for advice and services without realizing or understanding that your assistance or advice is something they should pay for, especially when it's for someone you don't know. If you can, calmly explain to your friend that this is how you earn your living and you can't afford to work without being paid for your time and expertise.

Response: "I wish I could assist your friend, but I simply don't have the time available right now."

Alert: Being accommodating does not pay the rent.

The Scenario

"You have to change your vacation. We need you at the year-end planning session."

What's going on here: You would like to attend this very important company event, but your vacation was blocked on the office calendar eight months ago—long before the session dates were posted. Your trip has been confirmed and expenses paid. You're important, but not essential. Yet you feel as if you might miss something or be missed. Canceling your vacation at this point is unreasonable, however, and the people you work for should understand.

Response: "I'm very torn, but I can't be there. I'll be sure someone is up-to-date and fully informed in my area to cover for me."

Alert: If you give in to the pressure and loyalty you feel, work will always take precedence over your personal time.

◯ *The Scenario*

"You have to tell me whether or not to take this job."

What's going on here: This person wants you to take the responsibility for his choices. Don't go there. If he takes the job and is content, he'll believe he made the decision himself. If he loathes the job, it will be your fault and you'll hear about it, possibly for a long time.

Response: "No, it has to be your decision."

Alert: In general you don't get credit for the good decisions you help people make, only blame for the ones that turn out poorly.

◯ *The Scenario*

"Can you come in over the weekend?"

What's going on here: The extra money is always enticing, but your partner or one of your children will be very unhappy. You've made plans that will need to be canceled or a promise you will need to break—to watch your child's soccer game or take her fishing, or to a movie.

Response: "I really can't."

Alert: It's very important to you and to those you love to honor your commitments to keep balance in your life. A life is best lived when balanced.

4

Really Difficult People

Saying no is daunting no matter who is asking, demanding, or badgering you. What's disconcerting is the fact that in many instances you can be more successful saying no to your boss or a meddlesome parent than to the person you hired to build a deck or color your hair—and hardly know. People whose job it is to sell their wares, close deals, or sign you up for a subscription come across as sure of themselves, so right or self-righteous that you become putty in their hands. Other times, their tenacity wears you down. Not every sales or service person is out to get you, but many are.

Forceful people make refusing feel as if you are trying to scale an icy cliff without the proper gear, slipping back with each step you take. When the belief that someone knows more than you do combines with the slightest personal insecurity, intimidation clouds your ability to be in control of what you want. The woman who owns the Wool Shop may crochet better than you do, but that doesn't mean she can dictate the color or style afghan that will look best in your home. Yet you may be inclined to go with her choice.

Half the time you agree because you think someone else has better taste or more experience. You allow yourself to be pressured and bullied; you don't speak up and end up feeling exasperated—mumbling to yourself later, "If only I had said no." It's time to practice saying no to those people who sway your decisions.

Selling You a Bill of Goods

Repair people dictate your schedule. Contractors tell you what to do, talk you into renovations you never considered. Salespeople are trained to sweet-talk (read *coerce*) you into owning things you don't necessarily need or have use for. When you get a purchase home, you're disappointed with it and with yourself. Common sense tells you to refuse, to hold firm, but you don't or can't. If and when you say no, the insistent don't hear you—or pretend they don't.

If there weren't something in it for them, they wouldn't be asking. You have to trust yourself and stick to your instincts to avoid being a patsy.

Knowing what you want and being informed about it will reduce your wavering. To overcome a salesperson's bravado, make it a point to be very direct. A forceful *no* gives you an edge, especially if it's unexpected, and leaves no room for fudging and second-guessing. You may notice the charm with which you were approached initially disappears and pushy people become more aggressive when confronted with *no*. As you strengthen your *no* skills, you'll find yourself less likely to take what's said at face value and more likely to understand when and how you are being conned.

The Scenario

"You look smashing in that color. It complements your eyes and gives you a vibrant glow. Shall I ring you up?" the cosmetician says as you pucker your lips and move closer to the mirror.

What's going on here: The striking young woman behind the makeup counter has just slathered a new color blush on your cheeks, a matching lipstick on your lips. You've never worn such a provocative color and are not convinced you look all that dazzling in spite of what the confident beauty consultant says. It's simply not you.

Response: "No."

Alert: Unlike a parent, friend, even a coworker, you don't owe salespeople an excuse or explanation, and you certainly don't have to worry about hurting their feelings. If you are the slightest bit unsure about the makeup, the probability is high that the new blush and lipstick will be stashed unused in the back of a drawer with the heap of cosmetics you were talked into every other time you didn't say no.

◯ The Scenario

"You'll be sorry you didn't buy this outfit. It's so versatile. It's what everyone is wearing," the salesperson in the sports department insists.

What's going on here: Her job is to sell you—and sell you big. She's the type who will tell you that you look great in a way-too-skimpy bathing suit. The buyer may have bought too much stock and the salesperson has been instructed to push some of the things you're trying on. She may work on commission; the more she sells, the fatter her paycheck. She spent a long time carting different sizes and colors to you in a dressing room. You feel a tad obligated to buy something.

Response: "No. I'm going to think about it."

Alert: It's her job to help you. It's okay to walk out of the store empty-handed. Before you're on the sidewalk, she'll be helping another customer. And on the remote chance that you *are* sorry you don't own the outfit, you can go back and buy it.

◯ The Scenario

"Sign this retainer and I'll get you the money you want and then some," the lawyer says with a knowing chuckle.

What's going on here: You want to believe that he can settle your case quickly for a lot of money and without a lengthy and stressful court trial. You suspect lawyer puffery, but are intimidated by the well-appointed office designed to make him feel like a giant and you feel like a midget. You know you should get another opinion, but how do you escape?

Response: "No, I want to think over what you're telling me." Or, "No, I'm going to see another lawyer before I decide."

Alert: Your radar should be working overtime when attorneys promise outcomes they can't predict and, for that reason, probably can't deliver either.

○ *The Scenario*

"It's ideal, just what you were looking for: enough bedrooms, good schools, large front and backyards. You can't let this house slip away," the realtor urges.

What's going on here: You've been house hunting for months. The agent wants to make a sale, and you want to find your dream house. This one isn't it, but it's close and very tempting. You flip-flop between compromising (you'll live with less closet space and spend the money to renovate the kitchen) and thinking you're being too picky. Maybe what you want just doesn't exist. You're relying on her experience and knowledge of the area. You could be swayed, especially when she informs you someone else has made an offer. You're also concerned that the realtor thinks you are being difficult.

Response: "Let's keep looking."

Alert: Don't worry about what the real estate agent thinks or be strong-armed by the pressure of another offer, and don't settle. You'll know when you find what you want and will happily make concessions.

The Scenario

"You have to drop your price if you want your house/apartment to sell."

What's going on here: You've studied the market and are very informed about the selling price of similar properties in the community. Given the age, condition, and location, your asking price is right and you're willing to wait. Your realtor isn't. The house isn't selling fast enough for him; he wants his commission now.

Response: "No, I'm holding out for my price. I'm confident I'll get it."

Alert: When you've done your homework and are convinced you are on target, stick to your guns. If circumstances change and you need the money in a hurry, you can reduce your asking price when you want, not when the agent wants.

The Scenario

The landscaper recommends you add three trees to the front yard plantings. "You won't be sorry. I know what I'm talking about," he adds to remind you that he's the authority on the space outside your home.

What's going on here: His original plan, however, called for one tree and a grouping of bushes. Feels like the old story—more of anything ups your bill. You like the first plan and wonder if he's correct. He's the supposed expert. What you really want to know is, if he's so good, why didn't he put three trees in the initial proposal? And what made him think you'll agree to pay hundreds of dollars more to an already expensive job?

Response: "No, I can add them later."

Alert: Trees grow, usually fairly rapidly. Wait a season to see how the spaces fill in. You probably won't need more trees.

The Scenario

"I've been watching this stock. It's as good as money in the bank. Should I buy you five hundred shares?"

What's going on here: Your broker has done pretty well by you overall. But he also has picked some dogs and promised gains that never materialized. Until you have time to do your own investigating, put him off.

Response: "Not yet. I want to look into it first."

Alert: Beware the sure thing. Nothing is for sure.

The Scenario

"Hi. I'm calling to update your information in your college alumni directory and offer you a copy."

What's going on here: Once you've confirmed that the caller is legit (by asking her to read what's listed under your name) and validated your entry, the sales pitch begins: you'll want to be able to get in touch with your classmates; the directory is a valuable business tool; you can't believe how useful it will be. The cost is negligible. What happened to the offer at the beginning of the conversation that made it sound as if she were giving you a copy?

Response: "No, thank you. I don't need the directory."

Alert: Read the fine print or ask a lot of questions. Who is publishing the directory? Does the money go to the college? Is the cost tax deductible? The majority of college alumni directories are put out by for-profit companies that have nothing to do with your alma mater.

The Scenario

"Everyone's ordering the navigational system. You can't buy a new car without one. You will be so happy you have it. You'll never be lost again."

What's going on here: You've ordered several extras, but the salesman pushes for another. If you've done your homework before car shopping, you know your automotive must-haves.

Response: "No, thank you. What's on the list is all I'm putting in this car."

Alert: Don't be conned by the "everyone has it" sales ploy.

◯ *The Scenario*

"We're going to highlight your hair today," the beautician declares emphatically as if it were a done deal.

What's going on here: On top of adding to your bill and her profit, maybe your stylist is having a slow day and wants to fill some time. Or maybe, just maybe, she really believes you will look better with highlights or with brown hair that's two shades darker. When you hesitate she takes it a step farther, "We talked about your becoming a blonde. Let's just do it," she pushes. You're not sure.

Response: "No, not today."

Alert: Even if a drastic change appears a good idea at the moment, to avoid total shock to your system or having to avoid seeing friends until you have the nerve to reveal what you've done, wait for your next appointment so you can give the transformation some thought to be certain it's what you want.

◯ *The Scenario*

"When are you going to start your package of ten training sessions?"

What's going on here: You just finished the second of two free sessions, a sign-up bonus for joining the gym. The package costs $250 and you feel obligated to the trainer, who worked hard with you. If you don't buy the package, you worry she gets nothing.

Response: "Not just yet. I'm going to wait to see how often I can get here."

Alert: The free sessions are "loss leaders," also known as "come-ons"—giveaways to bring you into the gym to spend more money. Unless you want a personal trainer and have the money, don't turn a good deal (free sessions) into a bad deal (ten sessions you don't need or can't really afford). The trainer is employed by the gym, so she's probably being paid for the time she's already spent with you.

◯ *The Scenario*

"This is the best holiday spot in the area. It's a bargain."

What's going on here: The travel agent arranged a very fabulous, very glamorous vacation, but you and the agent have a very different definition of the word *bargain*. The cost doesn't approximate the amount you mentioned, you have in your holiday budget, or would ever consider spending on a trip. Much as you would like to luxuriate on the remote island she selected and sip exotic drinks, you can't swing this extravagance.

Response: "No, it's too expensive."

Alert: Why do you care what a travel agent thinks about your net worth? Remind her of the figure you quoted or find another travel person to book your holiday. Or go online and book it yourself.

The Scenario

The dishwasher, the car, the television, the roof, the windows— "guaranteed for any and all breakdowns," the salesperson tells you.

What's going on here: If you were hesitant to make the purchase, when you hear the word *guarantee*, your resistance and doubt fade. With a guarantee you feel assured that the product will not give you any trouble. And if it does, it won't cost you anything to get it repaired. But why is the salesperson urging you to take the service contract?

Response: "If the product is guaranteed, why do I need a service contract?"

Alert: A lightbulb should go off in your head when you hear the word *guarantee*. Start asking questions yourself if your satisfaction is guaranteed and find out the store's return or replacement policy.

◯ *The Scenario*

"We only have a few left. Truthfully, I'd grab it if I were you."

What's going on here: The gizmo or gadget has caught on. It's getting harder and harder to find, but like most trendy items it will shortly become less expensive. Are you thinking of buying it because you need or like it, or because friends or neighbors own it? Could you be caught in the keeping-up-with-the-Joneses trap?

Response: "Thanks, but I'm going to wait until the price drops."

Alert: Be skeptical of the salesperson who uses any form of the words *honest* or *truth*. Remember that his job is to sell you.

Getting Things Done—Your Way

Telemarketers gobble your time, the babysitter runs your social calendar, the painter makes your color choices, the plumber comes when it's convenient for him, rarely accommodating your schedule. When you shrivel, you find yourself being taken advantage of or being bullied into decisions and results you're unhappy with. When you acquiesce, you feel angry, possibly enraged, for shying away from *no* and succumbing with a meek "okay."

Being tough is preferable when you want to have some control over the things you rely on others to do. They are trying to do their jobs, but too many aren't too concerned with how the outcome affects you. They proceed to the next job leaving you stewing or living with the consequences of going along with their suggestions. These questions, responses, and alerts, typical of situations you find yourself in at one time or another, will keep you from giving in to those people who can readily distress or disappoint you.

The Scenario

"We're doing a short telephone survey. I'd like to ask you a few questions; I'll only take a couple minutes of your time."

What's going on here: What happened to the government's no-call list? You signed up to be sure you were through with cold calls for good. Telemarketers and local public program callers ring your home anyway. They call when you're just sitting down to dinner or in the middle of your favorite television program and boldly inform you that the no-call list doesn't apply to them. Some ply you with the promise of a free trip or money if you'll just listen for a minute. You hesitate because you've always thought slamming down a phone in someone's ear was incredibly discourteous. Should you start to listen, the short pitch is long, the questions too personal or too many—many more than the "short survey" the caller claimed when you answered the phone.

Response: "No. Do not call here again." Or simply hang up.

Alert: Intrusive telemarketers and those who raise money for charities over the phone offer fertile ground for strengthening your *no* backbone. The chances of ever talking to the same person are minus-zero. If you can't say *no*, hang up the phone; the caller is being rude, not you.

⬤ *The Scenario*

"Hello, I'm calling from your local chapter of _____. We really need your support."

What's going on here: Local or not, worthwhile or not, unsolicited calls from people you don't know or charities not heading your donation list need to be discouraged. These days it's impossible to figure out what's a scam and what's for real. You could be making some schemer very rich if you buy his pitch.

Response: "No. Stop right there. I don't take telephone solicitations. Take me off your list."

Alert: Phone solicitations are an invasion of your privacy. Whatever they're offering or seeking is likely to be bogus.

⬤ *The Scenario*

"My guys are ready to start. My crew will arrive at eight-thirty tomorrow morning."

What's going on here: You've waited months for the contractor to give you a date, and out of the blue he'll be on your doorstep with almost no advance notice. What may have happened: his workmen suddenly had a free day and he has to pay them. Not your problem. It will take you half a day to clear out the area in which the work will be done, and you have a busy day scheduled away from the house. You're being bulldozed.

Response: "No, I need a few days warning."

Alert: He works for you. You are paying him. He's being unreasonable.

● *The Scenario*

"The color warms up the room, don't you think?"

What's going on here: Now that you see it, no, you don't think that. You think the opposite—the color is too deep, it's too sharp, too much contrast with your rug and furniture. Your instructions to the painter had been rather explicit: put a sample on the wall near the kitchen. He forged ahead and painted two walls before you saw it. He will try to convince you that you love it. He'll insist he can't change it—it's too dark, it's too late, the room is half done, we bought paint for the whole room—and will assure you that you'll get used to it. You'll have none of his placating. You should get what you asked for, and any reputable painter knows that.

Response: "No, it's not what I want. I can't live with it."

Alert: He's wrong; you are right. Don't back down. If you do, you will be reminded every time you enter the room of how you allowed him to browbeat you.

◯ *The Scenario*

The cable company tells you a repair person will be at your home between nine and five or eight and two or some other ridiculously long stretch.

What's going on here: The cable company thinks it owns your time—you'll wait six or more hours for the repair person and feel trapped all the while. If you have far more pressing things to do with your day or evening, ask the scheduler to do better with the time frame.

Response: "That's unacceptable. You will have to narrow the window of possibilities." (Some will try, so it's always worth a shot.)

Alert: It rarely hurts to be insistent, especially when you pay for monthly services. The company knows you can switch to the competition.

◯ *The Scenario*

"We need to operate immediately—within the next two weeks." The doctor frowns to underscore the urgency he feels.

What's going on here: You're scared and terrified by the illness and cowed by the doctor's experience and reputation. He was recommended by friends whose medical opinion you trust. They said he's the best in his specialty. But what if he's wrong? The symptoms are complicated and could mean a different diagnosis, one with cure options other than surgery. The doctor says he's positive his diagnosis is correct and tells you he has an opening in his surgery schedule for next Wednesday. You are meant to feel lucky that he can squeeze you in.

Response: "No, I want to get a second opinion. Unfortunately, I think it will agree with yours."

Alert: You've massaged his ego, so he'll welcome you back to schedule the surgery if that is your decision, but it will be an informed one. Competent, successful doctors usually don't object to patients consulting with other doctors.

● *The Scenario*

"Please add your social security number under your signature."

What's going on here: The moving company representative insists the company cannot hold your items in storage without your social security number. With identity theft rampant, you don't want your social security number on papers the movers will plop on the front seat of their truck for any- and everyone to see. You can't fathom why they need it. They will have all your precious possessions stored on their property, locked up so that even you can't get to them.

Response: "Absolutely not. Get your supervisor on the phone."

Alert: Going over someone's head may get the result you want.

○ *The Scenario*

You spot a platter and a pitcher in an antique store and decide you have to have it. The owner says, "I can't break up the set. The dishes match the platter and pitcher. We always sell this kind of item together. Do you want the whole thing?"

What's going on here: In large stores and chain stores there may be little room for bartering. Not necessarily the case in small shops. The clue here is the word *always*. He could have said, "We *never* break up sets" to deliver the same message. In life, there are exceptions. Walk away or be firm.

Response: "No. I don't want the set. I want those two pieces."

Alert: The words *always* and *never* are red flags. They're used as scare tactics to make you believe there's no room for negotiation. "Always" and "never" are fictional situations that don't exist; that may explain why we have the expression "never say never." When you no longer seem interested, you stand a better chance of walking out with what you want.

○ *The Scenario*

"Mrs. Cooke, I can't be at your house until seven-thirty on Saturday night," the babysitter claims.

What's going on here: You arranged seven with her weeks earlier. You need her, but you also need to be at a seven-thirty surprise party. She has you over a barrel— if you allow it. If the sitter arrives when she wants, you'll be a nervous wreck trying to get into the party without colliding with the guest of honor at the front door. Or you will have to wait until much later and miss the fun of seeing the shocked celebrant.

Response: "No, seven-thirty is unacceptable." Tell her why and remind her that you were quite clear about the time when you booked her.

Alert: This is a sanity-saving *no*. Don't be afraid to speak firmly; she'll be on time or find herself a replacement acceptable to you. She wants babysitting money as much as you want her, and she doesn't want you talking to her parents.

○ *The Scenario*

"Yes, we had a deal, but the parts cost more. Times are tough; I'm really hurting. I have to pay my employees."

What's going on here: This dealmaker has you marked as a softy. He'll embellish his sob story if you let him. Stories of financial woes push hard on the guilt buttons—and pull at your heart. He may or may not be deceiving you, but that is not the issue.

Response: "No, I'm not paying additional charges. We agreed on the price."

Alert: Stop whiners with an assertive *no* before they spill their sad stories and break your resolve.

CONCLUSION

Bowing Out

On the surface, saying no seems such a simple feat, but you understand the possible consequences—the feelings you might hurt, the career you might endanger, the friend who might dump you, the family you could divide, or the contractor who might walk off the job. You also know that being a yes-person wears you down and is equally risky.

Refusing is rarely easy, and sometimes it's downright uncomfortable, but saying yes habitually creates any combination of anxiety and anger, added stress, regret, and feelings of powerlessness. That's why it's important to keep your priorities straight, to know what *you* want, so you don't slip into trying to keep other people happy and forgoing your own needs.

If you expend too much energy looking for approval, worrying about how others perceive you, being a do-gooder, or overly compensating as payback to those who helped you,

you leave little time to take care of yourself—to rest, work out, read, see movies, play with your children, spend time with your partner, maybe fall in love. Just finding the right person requires a time investment and a commitment, too. In short, use available time to connect with those who make you laugh, who make you happy—time you won't have if you are at the beck and call of those who continually seek you out. Some, but not all of them, are self-centered.

When you understand that most people aren't thinking about you, aren't worrying about what you think, and many times are not concerned with how you will feel, you'll be less hesitant to say no. Store this thought in the back of your mind, but not too far back: *he or she is not thinking about me.* With that thought tucked away, you become discriminating about doling out assistance.

When a close family member is distraught or ill and needs support, you will want to extend yourself. When a friend is going through rough times or a colleague must tend to a personal crisis, a natural drive takes over and propels you to do what you can do. You'll be there to help in any way you can. Those special and extenuating circumstances should be exceptions, however, not part of the haphazard commitments and responsibilities you used to assume for everyone and everything.

You'll know when something feels right, when you want to do it. That desire should be as compelling as when you want to say no.

Finding the Courage

Keep your antenna up and running, on the alert for people who attempt to cross your boundaries. On hearing a request, if *no* runs through your mind, if instinctively that's how you want to respond, find the moxie to go with the feeling.

Consider the people you don't ask favors from and why you don't—probably because they have said no to you in the past. When you need strength or the incentive to say no, remember the friends, relatives, and coworkers who have little trouble saying no to you. Make them your benchmark, your source of courage. In spite of the times they failed to do a favor or turned down what you thought was a reasonable request, they remain in your inner circle. Most likely you still like, respect, or admire them. One or two refusals didn't turn them into monsters.

At this point have the courage to bow out gracefully, to retire your guilt, and feel good with every *no* you utter. Guilt is a wasted emotion; it eats up time and is almost never worth the wear and tear and drain on the psyche. Minus guilt, you'll be able to focus on critical and important responsibilities and to skip or ignore the unimportant. Your father isn't going to come home from work and punish you because you didn't do what Mom asked. (At least not anymore!)

No question you'll slip and say yes now and again when you don't mean to. If you return to your old ways, don't fret. After a relapse, there will be countless chances to get back on course and use your new skills.

The *No* Drill

You now have the ammunition to short-circuit those who believe it is their right to impose their demands on you. You've learned how, when, and why to reclaim *no* and put it back in your vocabulary, to make it the preferred response. That single word reduces stress levels and frees up time to enjoy life. You'll like yourself better when the days of being other people's scaffolding—their perpetual support system—are long gone.

The reality is, whatever you say yes to, at some point, will force you to say no to something and somebody else. When giving out time and services, be stingy and very selective so you can say yes to the person you truly want to assist. There will be times you simply can't wiggle out of something asked of you, but don't be hard on yourself. Make up your mind to say no to the next request, demand, or assumption that takes unfair advantage.

You now have a reservoir of different ways to say no and a better grasp of what and whom to say no to. You'll be able to stop the persuasive people who ask too much, too often. You've stopped volunteering indiscriminately and started to think about the other person's motive and about what you will get out of helping *before* you commit. Processing requests, that is, analyzing them before you jump into a *yes* response, will eliminate the inner conflict you feel after the fact and will help you turn down requests that build tension and squeeze time.

You know the drill and the warning signs. When you are assertive, people will hesitate before they seek you out.

Because most people don't like to be refused, they will avoid asking you. It's human nature. *No* is not magic—saying no is making a conscious effort to be in charge of your life. Begin today, if you haven't already. Keep track of whom you turned down, when, and why—and most significantly, how good it feels to make the right choices. Move yourself to the front of the line of people you want to please and keep happy.

Liberating Yourself

Saying no emphatically doesn't mean you are aggressive, obnoxious, selfish, or controlling, rather it means you know how to stand up for yourself. Yes, it is all about you: you being deceived, you giving your all and not getting much in return, you being smothered, controlled, or perpetually overworked, overextended, and tired.

Although it's easy to blame others for asking too much, you could be at fault for expecting too much of yourself. Exercise the option to choose, because in the world of *no*, reducing demands prevents you from choking on self-inflicted overload. Saying no is practicing self-defense, and that is not selfish.

Saying no offers instantaneous rewards; the most significant is the end of being a doormat masquerading as a person. Saying no lets you preserve time and choose how to spend it. You become free to move about the cabin that is your life and luxuriate in it.

It's liberating to be off the sucker list. But get used to and accept the idea that everyone can't love you.

Experiencing the Freedom

It's near impossible to keep one person happy, and keeping everyone happy is downright exhausting. When you try, your own dreams, your own fun, and your own happiness evaporate. On the other hand, when you stop being waylaid, you'll be proud, elated by the triumph, and oh so glad to have the burden and weight of incessant obligations lifted.

Once you accept the fact that being willing doesn't make you a better or more accomplished person, you'll be able to say no more readily. You can refuse an intrusive parent, a maniacal boss, an insistent child; you can say no to the favors that keep you scrambling and wondering how you'll get through the day. Calling up a *no* when it's needed is a supreme victory, one you will relish. You'll realize rather quickly that *no* is a gorgeous word.

A New Mind-Set

Your *no* education is your inoculation against the *yes* disease in its many forms. You've built immunity similar to that provided by a flu shot. The flu vaccine doesn't protect against all the strains of the virus, nor will this book inoculate you permanently. You will need reminders every so often.

Here are key lessons and insights in capsule form, booster shots, to assist you in saying no—and meaning it. When your resistance falters or you feel burdened, these thoughts and mantras will shore you up and get you to *no* successfully. They are crucial reinforcement to keep you focused on your goals and priorities so you can accomplish more of what you want and less of what others want from you. Repeat and reread them as needed:

* The first *no* to a person makes subsequent refusals easier.
* The word *no* is enough. Lengthy explanations leave wiggle room for debate, misinterpretation, or permission to ask again.
* Less is more. The less said in the way of excuses, the stronger the message. In other words, keep your mouth shut.
* Don't apologize for being unavailable.
* Be leery of statements and people who assume you consent.
* Be sure the person asking is in your friend, family, or elite work circle before considering how or if you want to comply.
* Having a reputation for being the person everyone leans on is not flattering and makes you a prime target for being railroaded into more yeses.

* If you're known for being able to juggle many tasks at once or for doing everything well, play down that myth. Being a star performer simply begets more requests.
* Anticipate what will be asked when you can. Thinking about possible situations that may arise ahead of time enables you to decide what you are willing to do and what you might delegate to someone else.
* Agreeing to do what others ask doesn't make you a nicer person.
* Being buttoned up, enthusiastic, or willing is great within limits, but don't overdo the image.
* You can't do enough for some people, don't try.
* You are not responsible for the problems others create for themselves, and you can't single-handedly make them happy.
* Upon hearing a request, immediately think, "No way." You can reconsider later.
* Dissect each request carefully to make sure you are not being bribed, cajoled, bullied, or threatened.
* Before agreeing to anything, ask yourself if you have the time.
* Be aware of your limits; reconsidering and redefining your boundaries will ease an escape.
* Believe that you can say no and remain an involved, caring, and committed person.
* Say no with conviction. Look the person in the eye to let him know you mean it, that appeals and pressure are useless.

* Don't fret over the consequences of refusing. If you've handled the situation well, the backlash will be absent or insignificant.
* Most people are understanding and forgiving. You don't want unforgiving people in your life anyway.
* Remind yourself daily that *no* is liberating and it's your right.

Tell me how you're doing with the *no* word. How has saying no more often changed your life? Your feelings about yourself? How others view you? Send me an update via www.thebookofno.com and check the site for periodic encouragement and new tips.
